OLD TODDINGTON REVISITED

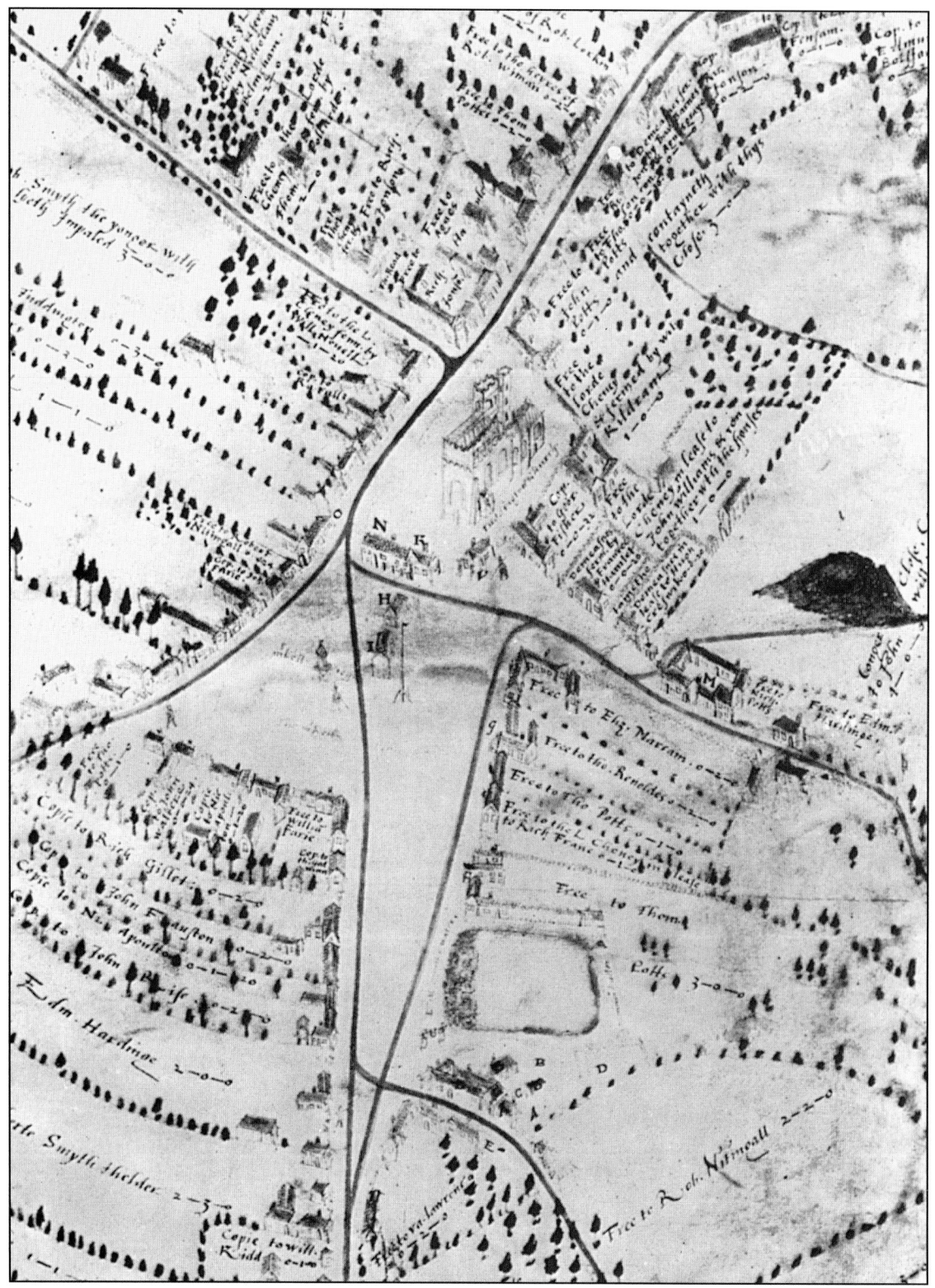

Toddington in 1581. Some of the buildings marked are: The Town House (N), The Town Kitchen (L), The Town Shambles (Butchers' Market) (I). Near the present site of Pett's garage is The Maypole. On the opposite side of the Green, on the site now occupied by the War Memorial is the 'Merket Cross'.

OLD TODDINGTON REVISITED

A Pictorial History of this Attractive Bedfordshire Village

Written and Researched
by
RICHARD HART

Copyright © Richard Hart

First published 1992

ISBN: 0 9511698 2 3

Printed by J.H.Haynes & Co Ltd

Published by Farnon Books
PO Box 248
Leighton Buzzard
Beds LU7 7JA

Acknowledgements

A book of this nature is essentially a patchwork put together from newspapers, books, photographs, postcards, reminiscences and memoirs. I am therefore indebted to the many authors of books and pamphlets and newspaper reporters who have written about Toddington over the last 150 years and thereby provided me with so much valued information. All efforts have been made to trace copyright holders of photographs and prose; but if any have been missed, the publisher would be pleased to include a suitable acknowledgement in any future editions.

I would like to take this opportunity to thank all those people who have lent me photographs, booklets and documents. In particular I wish to mention my wife, Jackie, and my parents, David and Priscilla, for their support and advice. I would like to thank David Morgan for allowing publication of his notes and Victor Seymour for permission to quote extracts from his book *Toddington Memories*. Finally, my thanks go to the *Bedfordshire Magazine*, Luton Museum and Art Gallery, Home Counties Newspapers Plc and *Kelly's Directory* for permission to reproduce copyright material.

The sources of the photographs and illustrations are as follows:

Author   14b, 18b, 20b, 21b, 22b, 23b, 24b, 25b, 26b, 27b, 28b, 29b, 32a, 33b, 37b, 44b, 45b, 49a, 70b
Bell's Photo Co   12b, 16ab
Blake and Edgar   18a, 29a
J.H. Blundell   frontispiece, 31a
Roy Bushby   69a
Cleaver   21a, 23a, 25a
Evening Post-Echo Ltd   68a
Howard Fletcher   52a
Christine Hart   42b, 47ab, 48b
David Hart   38a, 51ab, 53a
Priscilla Hart   68b
Claude Hawes   27a, 28a
Home Counties Newspapers Ltd   41b, 56ab, 58a, 61ab, 67a
Legge   41a,
Dr John Longstaff   49b
Luton Museum and Art Gallery   30b, 34ab, 54ab, 55ab, 57ab, 58b, 60ab, 62ab, 63ab, 64ab, 65ab, 66ab, 67b
Nancy Nicholls   50b
W.J. Roberts   31b
Arthur Simson   44a, 45a, 46ab, 48a
Charles Smy   14a, 36a

(a: above; b: below)

This book is dedicated to my parents
DAVID and PRISCILLA

List of Illustrations

Frontispiece: Map of Toddington in 1851

Page
- 8. Toddington in 1882
- 12a. View from church tower, 1920
- 12b. View from church tower, 1950
- 13a. Park Road, early 1900s
- 13b. View from church tower, early 1900s
- 14a. View from church tower, early 1900s
- 14b. View from church tower, 1983
- 15a. The Green in Victorian times
- 15b. The Green, about 1905
- 16a. The Green, 1940s
- 16b. The Green, 1940s
- 17a. High Street, about 1914
- 17b. High Street, about 1912
- 18a. High Street, 1900s
- 18b. High Street, 1983
- 19a. High Street, about 1910
- 19b. High Street, about 1950
- 20a. High Street, 1900s
- 20b. High Street, 1990
- 21a. High Street, 1930s
- 21b. High Street, 1990
- 22a. High Street, about 1900
- 22b. High Street, 1990
- 23a. High Street, 1930s
- 23b. High Street, 1990
- 24a. Dunstable Road, about 1940
- 24b. Dunstable Road, 1990
- 25a. Dunstable Road, 1930s
- 25b. Dunstable Road, 1990
- 26a. Park Road, 1920s
- 26b. Park Road, 1990
- 27a. Park Road, 1915
- 27b. Park Road, 1990
- 28a. Park Road, 1923
- 28b. Park Road, 1990
- 29a. Station Road, 1911
- 29b. Station Road, 1991
- 30a. War Memorial, 1920s
- 30b. Village pump, 1920s
- 31a. St George's Church, 1812
- 31b. St George's Church, 1902
- 32a. St George's Church, 1991.
- 32b. St George's Church, interior, 1900s
- 33a. Pond, 1900s
- 33b. Pond, 1991
- 34a. Conger Hill, 19th century
- 34b. Shrove Tuesday, 1940
- 35. Aerial view, 1964
- 36a. Toddington Manor
- 36b. Monmouth oak tree
- 37a. Old parsonage
- 37b. Water tower, 1983
- 38a. Neale, Baker & Co, about 1899
- 38b. Fish cart, about 1907
- 39a. Roadmen, 1930s
- 39b. Milk cart, about 1930
- 40a. Fire brigade, 1919
- 40b. Blacksmith, early 1900s
- 41a. Thatcher, 1990
- 41b. Brian Uridge, 1990

(a: above; b: below)

Page
- 42a. W.J.Hobbs, butcher, 1904
- 42b. Liz and Tim's, pet foods, 1974
- 43a. *Bell Inn*, about 1906
- 43b. George Hart's newsagents, 1925
- 44a. Nos 2, 4 and 6 High Street, 1970
- 44b. Nos 2 and 4 High Street, 1990
- 45a. Arthur Simson's shoe shop, 1970
- 45b. Bellingers bookshop, 1990
- 46a. W. McInerney, grocers, 1970
- 46b. Hi-Lites, 1970
- 47a. J.S. MacPherson & Co, 1970
- 47b. K & B greengrocers, 1970s
- 48a. P. & M.Williamson's draper's shop, 1970
- 48b. Barclays Bank, 1973
- 49a. Sampler by Phoebe Peach, 1878
- 49b. Staghounds, 1899
- 50a. Fair, early 1900s
- 50b. Toddington Stars, 1906
- 51a. Concert, about 1912
- 51b. Play, about 1913
- 52a. Social Club, about 1920
- 52b. Toddington bus, about 1923
- 53a. Seaside trip, 1930s
- 53b. Choir, about 1935
- 54a. Social Club, fifth birthday, 1950
- 54b. Darts league finals, 1953
- 55a. Toddlers' party, 1954
- 55b. Senior citizens' dinner, 1953
- 56a. Mothers' Union children's Christmas party, 1953
- 56b. Mothers' Union children's party, 1954
- 57a. Rovers football team, 1954
- 57b. Church Hallowe'en party, 1956
- 58a. Mothers' Union and Young Wives party, 1960
- 58b. Young Farmers' Club, speaking contest, 1961
- 59a. Primary School football team, 1961
- 59b. Primary School class, 1962
- 60a. Scouts gang show
- 60b. Opening of Parkfields School, 1963
- 61a. Parkfields play, 1963
- 61b. Church choir, 1960s
- 62a. Guessing the weight of the cake, 1965
- 62b. Maud Dunham and Beryl Hyde
- 63a. Mr and Mrs John Gibbs
- 63b. Mr H. Russell
- 64a. Social Club prize-winners, 1967
- 64b. Last day of Primary School, 1967
- 65a. Nativity play, 1967
- 65b. Opening of Crescent Court flats, 1967
- 66a. Christian Aid sponsored walk, 1968
- 66b. Army Cadets club opening, 1968
- 67a. Young Farmers play, 1968
- 67b. Primary School swimming pool, 1968
- 68a. Fred Ireland and Reg Marlow, 1979
- 68b. Consecration of new cemetery, 1990
- 69a. Best Kept Village award, 1990
- 69b. Dr John Longstaff
- 70a. Toddington Show advert, 1982
- 70a. Sir Neville Bowman-Shaw
- 70b. Dunstable Bowmen

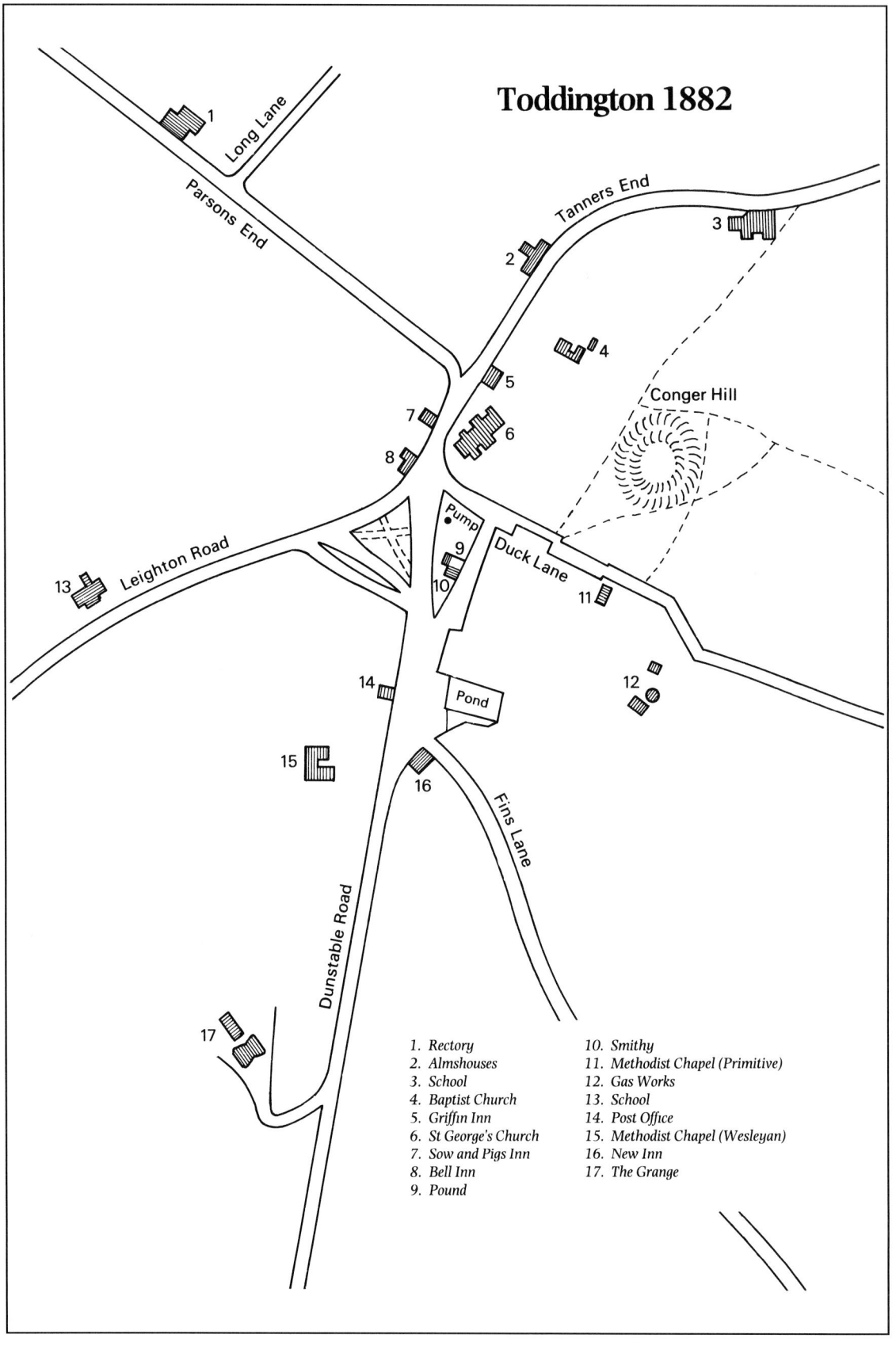

Contents

Introduction 10

Views from the Church Tower 12

The Green 15

High Street 17

Dunstable Road 24

Park Road 26

Station Road 29

Around the Village 30

People at Work 38

Businesses 42

Village Life 49

Toddington in 1892 71

Toddington Memories 78

Schooldays in the 1930s 81

Village Inns 83

Toddington in 1950 87

Education 89

Did You Know? 90

Kelly's Directory, 1940 94

Roll of Honour 96

Introduction

The village of Toddington is almost a small town, with a population of 4,240 in 1981. For hundreds of years the magnificent cruciform parish church of St George of England has overlooked and dominated the village green. Its rare three-storeyed parvise was originally used as a chapel and living quarters for the priest.

Wells and pumps supplied the drinking water in the village with the larger properties boasting a supply of their own. When mains supplies became available, some of the older villagers were reluctant to change over to the 'piped stuff'. The pond, which provided water for stock and travellers' horses, has now been turned into a memorial garden to the parishioners who gave their lives in the service of this country during the wars of 1914-18 and 1939-45.

The Green was used to graze the villagers' livestock, and houses built around it helped to form a compound to protect the animals from predators at night. Today the Green provides the decorative focal point of the village upon which five roads converge. Despite all the changes, the Green has managed to retain its charm and has helped the village to attract new residents.

In 1906 the following history of Toddington was published in *Kelly's Directory*:

TODDINGTON is a large parish and ancient market town, $2\frac{1}{2}$ miles south-west from the Harlington station of the main line of the Midland railway, about $5\frac{3}{4}$ south-east from Woburn and 15 south from Bedford, in the Southern division of the county, hundred of Manshead, Woburn petty sessional division, Ampthill union, country court district of Leighton Buzzard, rural deanery of Dunstable, archdeaconry of Bedford and diocese of Ely. The town has an ancient appearance and is very irregularly built. The parish is lighted with gas from works opened December 21, 1863. The Flitt, a tributary of the Ivel, flows through the parish.

The church of St George is a noble cruciform structure, chiefly in the Early English and Perpendicular styles, consisting of chancel, with sacristy of two storeys, clerestoried nave of four bays, aisles, transepts, south porch, and a central embattled tower of three stages, with angle turret, and containing a clock, with chimes, erected during 1862-75 and 8 bells, originally all cast in 1792, but in 1906 5 bells were re-cast and 3 re-tuned, at a cost of £500 and the whole rehung; there is also a sanctus bell, dated 1665: the nave arcades and the lower stage of the tower are Early English; the upper stage, aisle and clerestory, Perpendicular: the north aisle and transept, as well as the vestry, have a singular cornice, highly enriched with grotesque figures of human beings, beasts and birds: the roof displays elaborately carved figures of angels holding shields, wreaths, and other ornaments: in the south transept, under an arched recess in the south wall, are two tombs with recumbent effigies of marble, the western-most being that of a knight in armour, with surcoat of his arms, and on either side an angel holding across his breast an inscribed scroll; the figure represents Thomas Peyvre, 1429, a descendant of Paulinus Peyvre, who held the manor in the reign of Henry III; the other effigy is that of a female in mantle and richly jewelled wreath, representing Margaret (Loring), wife of the preceding Thomas; the inscriptions, now lost, are given in Cott. MSS. Cleop. c. iii f.8, Brit. Mus.: against the west wall is the cross-legged effigy of a knight with the arms of Peyvre on his surcoat, supposed to represent Nicolas Peyvre, 1361-2, father of the above: another tomb, the sides of which are adorned with shields of arms, is inscribed to Anne (Broughton), 1561, wife of Sir Thomas Cheney kt. K G lord warden of the Cinque Ports; the next is an alabaster tomb, now much mutilated and partly of brick, with an effigy in rich armour of Henry Cheney, baron Cheney of Toddington, 1587, son of the foregoing; and one more tomb bears the effigy of his wife Jane (Wentworth), 1614, attired in wimple and mantle: in the north transept are several tombs of the Wentworth family, who held the manor in the 17th and 18th centuries, including one erected at a cost of £2,000, to Henrietta Maria, baroness Wentworth, 1686, daughter and sole heir of Thomas, Lord Wentworth and Philadelphia (Cary) his wife, both of whom, as well as Thomas, earl of Cleveland, are interred beneath: on the opposite side is a large canopied mural monument to Maria, 1632, eldest daughter of Thomas, earl of Cleveland, and Ann (Crofts) his wife; here are also buried William, 1623, and Charles, 1622, sons of the same peer: in the chancel is a monument to Gyles Bruse esq. 1594, youngest son of Sir John Bruse, of Great Wenham, Suffolk kt. placed by his sister Alice, his tomb, with inscription, being under the chancel arch; there are also brasses to Thomas Claver, rector, 1654; and Thomas Pennington, gent. 1643, and some fragments: King James I attended divine service in this church on the 24th July, 1608: a portion of the fabric was restored, at a cost of about £3,000, by the Rev John Clegg MA rector 1862-75, and the Rev C. E. Haslam, rector 1876-86, and during the year 1893 further restoration was carried out, at an additional cost of nearly £1,000; and in the course of the work, during the period 1862-86, several mural paintings were discovered on both sides of the nave and over the north door: there are sittings for 750 persons.

The register dates from 1540, and is in a fair state of preservation; the 4th vol. contains a large and interesting collection of Briefs from 1653 to 1810. The living is a rectory, yearly value £580, including 206 acres of glebe, with residence, in the gift of Mrs Pipon, and held since 1901 by the Rev James Clement Collier Pipon MA of Lincoln College, Oxford, and hon. minor canon of Chester cathedral. Abraham Hartwell, rector here, according to Lysons, in the 17th century, was a learned writer of that period, and bequeathed his library for the use of his successors. Here are places of worship for Baptists, Wesleyans and Primitive Methodists; the Wesleyans have day and Sunday schools here. A cemetery of 1 acre 3 roods was formed in 1856, and is under the control of the Parish Council. A Reading Room was established in 1897. The straw plait manufacture is carried on here to some extent. There is a fire brigade, consisting of one superintendent and 12 firemen, and the engine house is in the Church square. The market was originally held on Thursday, but was changed to Saturday by a charter of King Edward II in 1316. Fairs are held on April 25th, the first Monday in June, November 2nd and December 6th, and a statute fair on the Wednesday before Old Michaelmas Day.

Toddington Hospital, founded (in 1443) by John Broughton, for a warden and three poor men, and dedicated to St John the Baptist, was dissolved by Sir Thomas Cheney, and subsequently seized by the Crown. The charity estate, comprising a small farm and house, produces about £60 yearly, and is administered by trustees; a charge on Herne farm of £20 a year is for three widows. In a field belonging to the late William Harbett esq. in this parish, a variety of antiquities, viz. black earthen pots filled with small bones, also spear heads, swords and iron helmets, have been found. This place was the seat of Sir Paulinus Peyvre, who was steward of the royal household of Henry III and erected here a fine manor house; here also resided in the reign of Henry VIII Sir Thomas Cheney KG and his son Sir Henry Cheney kt. afterwards Baron Cheney of Toddington; the latter built a magnificent residence here, about half a mile from the church, forming a quadrangle 210 feet on the north and south sides; it was at one time the residence of Henrietta Maria Baroness Wentworth. Mrs Warren-Vernon, lady of the manor and principal landowner, resides at Toddington Park; the Manor House being now (1906) unoccupied. The grounds, covering about 25 acres, are let with the manor. The soil is marl and clay; subsoil, gravel. The chief crops are wheat, barley, oats, beans and peas. The area is about 5,528 acres of land and 7 of water; rateable value, £14,099; the population in 1901 was 1,962.

Views from the Church Tower

Above: 1920s view from the church tower. Note the condition of the Green. Traffic was not unknown to track its way over the Green's unlevel surface, cutting it up and thereby making it even more unsightly.

Below: The same view 30 years later. In 1938 the Coronation Committee restored beauty to the Green by planting shrubs and trees on it. The County Council dumped many tons of earth on it in order to make it level. The council also laid white concrete kerbstones and made up the footpaths.

Park Road, early 20th century. X marks the spot of the residence known as Coelwolf (formerly Wythingtons). Wainholm can clearly be seen centre right. At one time Wainholm was the headquarters of a carrier of corn from Toddington to London.

Early 1900s view looking across the Green, with a fair in the foreground. Note the letters BANK on the High Street corner property. Except in the City of London, hanging signs were not widely used in this country until the late 1920s.

Above: Early 1900s view of Market Square. The fenced compound behind the smithy on the right is the village pound, where stray animals were kept until claimed.

Below: In this modern picture the library (left) has replaced Clifford's bakery shop. The pound and smithy have been replaced by an electricity substation and garage. Fairs are no longer allowed on the Green.

The Green

The Green in late Victorian times. In about 1887 a report by G. Culley said: 'I shall never forget the scene I witnessed when accompanying the Relieving Officer on one of his weekly visits to Toddington where a large proportion of the male population of so-called workmen expect the female plaiters to maintain them throughout a great proportion of the year. At the time of my visit one third of the entire population of the parish were receiving relief, and it seemed to altogether puzzle the Relieving Officer to account for the manner in which one half of the remainder lived.'

The village green, about 1905. The roads are unmettled and very dusty and stony in summer and muddy in winter. Note the wooden signpost and gas lamp near the church wall.

Above and Below: The Green in the 1940s. The wooden bell tower on top of the Town Hall (above) housed the fire bell. In order to ring this someone had to get the key of the hall, unlock the door, and pull the bell rope which hung inside. The problem was often to know where the key was, as either someone hadn't replaced it, or the holder was not at home.

High Street

High Street, about 1914. The pole on the left is outside Edwin Drewe's barber's shop, where the cost of a haircut was twopence. Sharing the same entrance was Ellen Drewe's newsagent's shop, where children would buy comics such as Chips together with marbles, tops and penny boxes of paint. Adjacent to the barber's shop was Julia Pitts', general draper's. Next door (partly obscured by the horse and cart) are the premises of Alex Horley, grocer, tax collector and insurance agent.

High Street, about 1912. Note the pond on the right and the traffic-free road.

Above: 1900s view with the bank on the corner (Barclay & Company Limited, sub-branch, open on Saturdays only, 11 am to 2 pm). A couple of doors away is the Queen's Head *inn with the sign 'stabling'.*

Below: This 1983 picture shows the many changes that have occurred. Note that the Queen's Head *has now become Balfours newsagent's shop. Barclays Bank have moved to Market Square and their former premises are now for sale.*

Above: High Street, about 1910. A group of boys are outside 'Tubby' Burnett's sweetshop, which was kept by a brother and sister, Henry and Miss Burnett. Apparently they had 'a sharp tongue with little love for children except their ha'pence'. The premises are now occupied by Halifax Property Services.

Below: A similar view some 40 years later. Note the telephone box outside the newsagent's shop. It was put there in the 1930s and moved to its present site opposite the post office in the 1950s.

Above: On the right, the premises of Richard and John Pilgrim, wheelwrights, can be seen with 'a much tarred boarded wall, shuttered windows facing the road and a thatched roof overhanging the path and dripping wet on all the passers-by. It had two large doors and an entrance large enough for farm carts and even elevators to enter. The inside of the doors, where paint brushes had been wiped off, were as many-coloured as Joseph's coat, the chief colours being the reds and blues used in the painting of farm implements'.

Below: Some 90 years later the premises have been pulled down and the site is occupied by T.M. Tyre and Exhaust Services Ltd.

Above: This picture was taken some 60 years ago. The window blind shades the window of Mr Cleaver's sweetshop (now Scallywags). Next door at No. 24 are the premises of George Allen and Son, plumbers and glaziers.

Below: This modern view shows the omnipresent motor car, which has replaced the horse and bicycle as the main means of transport.

Above: High Street about 1900 with the Hare *inn on the left selling Bennett's fine ales.*

Below: Today the inn has become a private house.

Above: The top end of the High Street in the 1930s. The warehouse and the white house known as The Lawns have been replaced by Grange Gardens. The warehouse was a large building which was used as a store for corn, flour and hay. The floor was raised a yard above the road to enable carts to unload when backed up to the double doors.

Below: Modern view. Note the introduction of lampposts, kerbstones, white lines and television aerials.

Dunstable Road

Above and Below: Some 40 years separate these pictures of Dunstable Road. Note the absence of street lighting in the picture above. The junction with Princess Street is centre right. The view below was taken in 1990.

The 1930s view of Dunstable Road shows a grass verge and no kerbstones. Note the absence of traffic and compare this with the modern picture, below, taken on a 'quiet' Sunday in 1990.

Park Road

Above: Park Road in the 1920s, with a horse and cart making its way slowly along the dirt track. The old vicarage can be seen on the right. It is interesting to note that the old name for Park Road was Parson's End.

Below: A 1990 picture with not one motor car in view – a rare sight!

Above: Park Road, 1915. Claude Hawes and Victor Seymour with metal hoop stand by the huge elm tree.

Below: This same view taken 75 years later shows the changes that have occurred. Manor Road is on the left.

Above: Park Road, 1923, looking towards the house called Clearview. The flock of sheep are standing near the junction with Manor Road.

Below: 1990s view.

Station Road

Above: This 1911 postcard looks along Station Road towards the post office (X). In the foreground George Moore's hairdressing shop can be seen, with Alfie Ruffet's motor repair and cycle shop next door.

Below: A similar view some 80 years later.

Around the Village

The War Memorial, surrounded by railings, late 1920s. The memorial was open on Saturday and Sunday afternoons for the laying of flowers.

The water pump, which stands on the Green, was presented to the village in 1855 by the Lord of the Manor, W. Dodge Cooper. When mains water was eventually made available, some of the older villagers were reluctant to change over to the 'piped stuff'. Picture taken in the 1920s with Mr Groom at the pump.

Above: St George's Parish Church, 1812. The Tollbooth and Sessions House are on the left whilst the building known as the Town Kitchens is on the right. The latter, which stood in front of Conger House, is stated to have accommodated ten families. It was pulled down in 1828.

Below: 90 years later, the Tollbooth and Sessions House have gone. The lean-to, where the fire engine was kept, can be seen on the left.

Above: Modern view of the church, village green and pump.

Below: Interior of the church, early 1900s. Note the manorial pew (left), installed in the 1820s.

Above: The pond has been a feature of the village for centuries and can be seen on a 1581 map as the 'Towne Water'. The water was used by local children for bathing; and before the 1914-18 war, horses and carts used to go down a blue brick ramp into the pond to cool the horses and swell the cartwheels in order to tighten them up.

Below: More than 90 years separate these views. Today all the houses seen in the earlier picture have gone. The area of water today is much smaller and no one would think of taking a morning swim in it! The pond is surrounded by the Memorial Gardens and bears a plaque to the educationalist Sir Frederick Mander, who lived in the village for a while. He was General Secretary and President of the NUT, and Chairman of Bedfordshire County Council.

This drawing shows Conger Hill, as it was in the 19th century. This prominent earthwork is situated near the church. Its origin is obscure, as it has never been excavated. One popular theory is that it was a fort. With its commanding position at the top of the hill, it would have formed a good line of defence against the invading Saxons.

Shrove Tuesday, 1940, with schoolchildren lying down listening to the Old Woman frying pancakes beneath the mound. Television news cameras have attended on several such occasions since this date.

Aerial view with Conger Hill in the foreground, 1964.

Toddington Manor, first quarter of this century. It was once the fifth largest great house in Bedfordshire. In 1671 Woburn Abbey had 82 hearths, whilst Luton Hoo, Houghton House and Wrest Park had 60, 55, and 52 hearths respectively, compared with 45 hearths at Toddington Manor. The greater part of the house, which was built about 1545, was pulled down by Lord Stafford in 1745 after it had fallen into decay, leaving one original turret, kitchen and stables. The turret became a staircase and the kitchen became a dining hall. The Manor House was visited twice by Queen Elizabeth I and once each by James I and Charles I. Today Sir Neville and Lady Bowman-Shaw live here.

The Duke of Monmouth and Henrietta Wentworth were lovers who walked and hunted in the grounds of the Manor. Amid the rolling parkland, the fish ponds, dovecotes, tennis courts and orchards they found this oak tree where they carved their initials. Today that oak still stands and although the initials are indecipherable, owing to growth of the tree, traces of them can still be seen.

Old parsonage in Park Road. This building pictured in the 1930s was intended to house a large family. It was very damp and draughty and was demolished in the 1960s. A new vicarage was built in the 1950s, in Leighton Road.

This monstrosity was built to supply water to the village. Situated in Leighton Road, it was demolished in the late 1980s.

People at Work

Neale, Baker & Co, the High Street bakers, with Arthur Neale and his wife, Martha, about 1899. The grating and windows of the cellar bakehouse can be seen.

Two brothers from Leagrave with a basket in hand stand by their horse and cart. They used to deliver fish to the local residents. One of the brothers was known as 'Old Skip'. Picture taken about 1907.

Roadmen – A. Clark, W. Smith, H. Evans and H. Aldred – at the top end of the High Street tarring the road, 1930s.

A horse and cart with milk churn turn into the Manor drive. Note the thatched roof of Manor Lodge. Picture taken about 1930. Milk would be delivered each day by horse and cart. The milk was transferred by tap from a big churn into a large delivery can, and then measured out in half pints and pints into the customers' jugs at their back door. A plunger was used in the churn to make sure the cream of the milk was evenly distributed.

Toddington Fire Brigade, taken at the Peace Day celebration, 19 July 1919, with the 1832 fire engine known as 'The Merry Widow'. The fire engine had two handles, one at each side, which could be worked alternately up and down by six or eight men, forcing the water through the hose. Some of the people pictured include: Mr. Nicholls, Billy Neal, Owen Pilgrim, Harry Evans, Eddy Muckleston, Charlie Joy, Harry Holman with coalman Fred Taylor holding the horse's head.

The village blacksmith, early 1900s. The sign on the shed reads 'J Pett RSS. general smith. All kinds of repairs neatly executed'. The modern equivalent of the smithy is the garage. It is therefore no surprise to find that this blacksmith's has now become the Old Forge Garage. It is still run by the Pett family, with Ivor Pett in charge.

Thatcher Nick Mackay puts the finishing touches to a 400-year-old barn in Park Road, 1990. The building, which is now in use as offices, was last re-roofed 40 years ago. To thatch a roof these days costs between £5 and £7 a square foot compared with £4 a square foot for modern concrete tiles.

Brian Uridge, with the front page of the Bucks Advertiser *that carried the story of the Great Train Robbery (1963), pictured on his retirement as* Luton News *reporter in 1990. He spent 43 years in journalism – 33 of them with the Home Counties Newspapers group.*

Businesses

Above: This postcard dated 1904 advertises the shop of 'W. J. Hobbs, butcher and licensed dealer in game'. Note the pigs hanging from the wooden frames outside the shop.

Below: The same shop some 70 years later. The board above the shop reads: 'Liz & Tim's Sunny Bank Pet Foods and Accessories'.

View of the Bell inn (left), about 1906, selling Aylesbury Brewery Company's celebrated ales; the post office; and the Sow and Pigs inn, where 'good stabling' could be obtained. Miss Ashby, the postmistress, would appear at the doors of the post office with a telegram in hand and blow her whistle. The telegrams were delivered by boys or characters such as 'Brown Joe' or 'Little Edwin' for threepence or sixpence, depending upon the distance involved.

George Hart's newsagent's shop (left), 1925, advertises the film The Timber Wolf, *showing at the local cinema, the* Picturedrome *in Gas Street (Conger Lane). The cinema was open twice weekly and George was often seen dashing across the Green in order to open the* Picturedrome.

Above: Nos. 2, 4, & 6 High Street in 1970.

Below: 20 years later, Richard's hairdressers and Barclays Bank have become, respectively, Ennerdale Travel and Toddington Insurance Services.

Above: Simson for Shoes with a private house next door (left), 1970.

Below: 20 years later this modern picture shows the shoeshop has now become Bellingers, selling books, gifts and pine furniture. The private residence has now become Rowe and Co.

This lovely old shop, W. McInerney, grocers, pictured in 1970 has been demolished to make way for Marlborough Place.

Hi-Lites, lighting specialists and fabric shade makers, 13 Market Square. Next door is V.I. Buckingham, butcher and grocer, 1970.

The estate agents, J. S. MacPherson & Co, pictured in 1970. The agency is now part of Halifax Property Services.

K and B, greengrocers, 1970s.

P. and M. Williamson's general and fancy drapers shop, 1970. This must be the only shop in Toddington that has not changed since it opened in the 1930s. If you want to step back in time and sample some old-fashioned service, it is well worth a visit.

Barclays Bank at 2 High Street in 1973. It moved in the 1980s to Market Square.

Village Life

Sampler loaned by Parkfields School, at the St George of England Flower Festival, 1990. This sampler was made by Phoebe Peach, who was the school caretaker for many years. She was born on 25 January 1868 and was admitted to the National School at the age of three in February 1871. Phoebe was ten when she completed the sampler.

Col A.P. Somerset's staghounds on the Green, 9 March 1899. The Town Hall, in the background, is in the process of having an external staircase built on.

Fairs came regularly to the village. Their decorated wagons, drawn by piebald horses, would come to the meeting place on the Green. Victor Seymour recalls: 'Some had a wicker-work crate at the back with half a dozen or so chickens in. These were then let loose as soon as they had shut the horse out of the shafts and staked him down at the end of a piece of rope to graze, but they rarely strayed far from the caravan to which they belonged!'

Toddington Stars, 1906.
Back row: Cecil Briden, Fred Ireland, Charlie Muckleston, Dick Clark, Harry Cleaver. Middle row: Ernest Brazier, Erskine Page, Harry Randall Front row: Billy Horley, Reg Neale, Stan Page, Albert Osborne, Jack Smith ('Pimp')
The club was formed in the 1890s and today is known as Toddington Rovers. It is one of four surviving original members of the Beds FA.

Above: Concerts were held regularly for various causes. Performances are said to have been of a high standard. Picture taken, 1912.

Below: Miss Hopwood, a local resident, wrote several plays that were performed in the open air in Toddington. They were called 'pastoral absurdities' and were advertised by striking, hand-painted posters. The parts were all played by local residents This picture of the cast of St George and the Dragon *was taken about 1913.*

Toddington Social Club, 6 High Street, 1920. The Social Club, which was available to people over 16 years of age. had a billiards table and a table for draughts, cards and dominoes. Pictured are: Rupert Fletcher, – , Tom Tilzey (the caretaker, standing in doorway), Jack Marlow, Mr Garner, Jack Randel, Dickie Dyer, George Hobbs and Ted Row.

The first National bus service, which ran from Toddington to Luton via Fancott, Chalton and Leagrave. The fare for a six-day weekly season ticket was 4s 6d and the conductor, Archie Hart, used to shout 'Heads down, mind the bridge!' as the bus went under the Leagrave railway bridge, about 1923.

If you were lucky, a holiday in the 1930s would be a trip to the seaside with aunts, uncles and cousins plus the family servant. Few families had a car, however, and for most people holidays away at the seaside were not an option. Pictured are: William Williamson, Jenny Wooliscroft, Dora Williamson, Martha Hart, Ella Hart, Minnie Neale, Reg Neale. The children are: David Hart, Pat Williamson, Molly Williamson and Doreen Neale.

Toddington Church Choir, about 1935. Toddington Church won the shield for choir singing in a competition held at Leighton Buzzard. Some of the people pictured include: Nellie Lane, Laurie Muckleston and Miss Dunham. Toddington's rector, Rev F.W. Hunt, is seated next to the rector of Leighton Buzzard with Bruce Wootton, choirmaster, on his right.

The Social Club celebrate their fifth birthday at a special supper held in the club, May 1950.

Sir Frederick Mander presents the Darts Pairs Trophy to A. Goodship (centre) and T. Claridge at Toddington Darts League Finals in the United Services Club, May 1953.

Toddington toddlers enjoying a party in the Social Club as guests of the Infant Welfare Centre, January 1954.

Many Toddington senior citizens are here as guests of the Women's Institute at a special dinner, held in October 1953.

Mothers' Union Christmas party for children, 1953. Back row: Mrs Palmer, – , Barry O'Dell, Priscilla Hart with Richard, Mary Mountfort with Mary Elizabeth. Front row: Daphne Muckleston, –, –, Sheila O'Dell, Andy Palmer, Marlene Palmer, James Biggs, Joanna Harris, Leslie Hyde.

Mothers' Union children's party, 1954, in the club room, Park Road. Among the adults pictured are: Bessie O'Dell, Marie Hiscock, June Cowper, Mrs Biggs, Mrs Bryant, Rev S. Fell, Mrs Palmer, Joan Harris, Mrs Fell, Mary Mountfort, Mrs Briden, Priscilla Hart. The children include: Mary Mountfort, Sheila O'Dell, Daphne Muckleston, Marlene Palmer, James Biggs, Richard Bryant, John Bryant, Richard Hart, baby Cowper, Andy Palmer, Linda Hiscock, Robert Cowper, Joanne Harris.

Toddington Rovers football team, 1954.

Church Hallow'een party, 1956.

Mothers' Union and Young Wives Christmas party, January 1960. Some of the people pictured are: Gwen Randall, Bessie Brazier, Priscilla Hart, Doris Dennis, Joan Marlow, Margaret Jays, Molly Woodfield, Marie Hiscock, Pam Saunders, Olive Chapmen, Bessie O'Dell, Gladys Parrott, Catherine Gravelle, Mrs Johnson, Kitty Stanghon, Dot Simson, Bertha Hyde, Lila Webb, Glenis Turner, Edie Crease, Dot Bryant and Jean Compton.

Toddington Young Farmers' Club teams who won the public-speaking contest against other YFC teams from Bedfordshire County. Standing (senior team): Vernon Burley, Jean Galloway, Jane Heady, Tony Poole. Seated: (junior team): John Little, Wendy Brooker, Susan Lay, Martin Edwards, March 1961.

Toddington Voluntary Primary School second football team, 1961, with Richard Dillingham, headmaster.

Toddington Voluntary Primary School, Class 1, July 1962. The teacher is Mr Lamb.

Scouts gang show, 1963.

Pupils and parents at the official opening of Parkfields Secondary Modern School, Wednesday, 16 October, 1963. The school was built at a cost of £136,000 by Messrs J.K. Hill and Sons (Ampthill) Ltd. Sir Frederick Mander officially opened the school and prizes were presented by Lady Mander. Victor Seymour presented the William Hyde Awards. Votes of thanks were given by John Wilson and Marilyn Mort.

The cast of Merchant of Venice, performed by pupils of Parkfields School, December 1963.

Toddington Choir in the 1960s.

Mrs R Joy tries to guess the weight of a cake at the Toddington Conservative Fete, September 1965.

Members present a clock to Mrs Beryl Hyde in appreciation of her nine years as President of Toddington Women's Institute. Miss Maud Dunham (left), a founder member, makes the presentation, December 1965.

Mr & Mrs John Gibbs, who opened the Baptist Church bazaar, November 1966, look at one of the stalls. Looking on are Mr M. Pope (church secretary), Rev G. Powell (the minister), Mrs Powell and little Alyson Powell.

H. Russell, a well-known Toddingtonian who occupied many posts in the church and social life of the village including that of church warden, vice chairman of the parish council and school manager. He opened the Church Fayre in December 1966. Little Mark Meadows, two and a half years old, grandson of the rector, Rev W.A. Bevis, is pictured on the knee of Mr Russell. Over £183 was raised at this event.

Successful competitors display their trophies at the Social Club Indoor Games Prize Presentation and Dinner, April 1967. Above are Mrs Gerard, Skittles Mixed Doubles runner-up; Mrs Ida Squires, Ladies Single Skittles winner and Mrs A Stevenson, Ladies Skittles runner-up.

Last day at Toddington Primary School, Station Road, July 1967. Parents wait outside for their children, who next term will move into a new school in Manor Road.

The cast of a Nativity play presented by the seven-year-olds of the infant department of the Primary School, December 1967. The class teacher was Mary Mountfort.

Official opening of the old people's flats at Crescent Court, December 1967. The building was opened by County Ald Mrs Alice Unwin and contains 28 bed-sitting room flats and four one-bedroomed flats for married couples. Present at the opening were the Luton RDC chairman, Cllr Tom Strange and the chairman of the Housing Committee, Cllr R. Clark and Cllr S.C. Clarke, chairman of Houghton Regis Parish Council.

Christian Aid sponsored walk, May 1968. Some of the 61 starters are seen here after passing checkpoint No 1 at Fancott. Included in this group is John Armstrong (extreme right). Over 50 people finished the 17 rainswept miles to a peal from the church bells. It was estimated that £100 would be raised if all the sponsors paid up.

In February 1968 the Army Cadet Unit Club's new hut in Luton Road was officially opened by Col Scott Clark, secretary of the Beds Army Cadet Force. Watched by the colonel, members can be seen here practising with a Bren gun.

An evening of one-act plays in May 1968 at Parkfields School saw the Young Farmers perform The Last Straw. Standing are: Brian Compton, Angela Watson, Andrew Howell and Richard Hart; seated: Mary Mountfort and Sally Abbiss.

Children of St George of England Primary School take full advantage of their new swimming pool during the brief snatches of summer weather, June 1968. Pictured are: Paul Livemore, Peter Gadsden, Philip Compton, Martin Northall, Haydn Richards, Tony Raggett, Tony Sinfield, Brian Weatherly, Neal Hewison, Christopher Webster, David Cook, Peter Spinlove, Mark Thorniwell, Susan Dart, Angela Tutt, Amanda Brewer, Christine Hart, Vanessa Edwins, Martin Webb, Peter Highnum.

Farmers Fred Ireland and Reg Marlow use a 42-year-old sheaf binder that enables straw to be cut in the traditional way, 1979. The straw is to be used for thatching.

Ceremony consecrating a new piece of ground for burials at Toddington Cemetery, April 1990. Rev Tony Knox is holding the staff for the Bishop of Bedford, who is performing the consecration. It is interesting to note that the church has made provisions for non-Christians by leaving one tenth of the ground unconsecrated.

Best Kept Village awards, 1990. Fred Simms (second from left) presents a certificate to David Thompson, of Flitwick. John Harfield, of Harlington (left), displays his certificate together with Chris Day (right), who received certificates on behalf of Toddington and Chalton.

Retired GP and former parish councillor Dr John Longstaff displays his wind-up gramophone on his allotment on which he plays records. His idea that plants respond to music was featured in the Daily Mirror. He told a Luton News reporter in 1990: 'I have been using it for the past two seasons and, despite the dry summer, I have had a very good crop.'

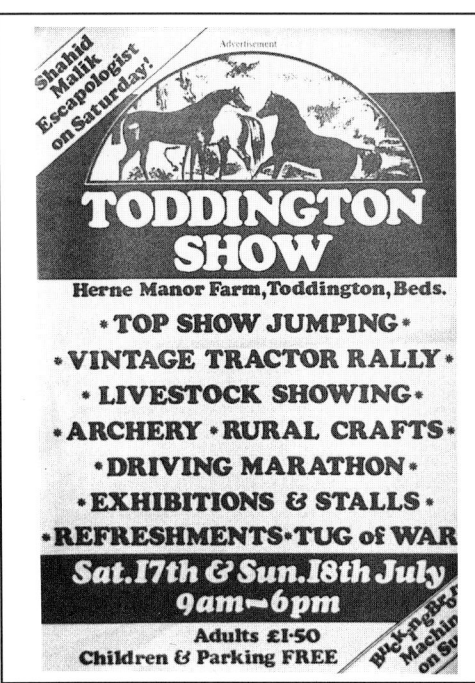

Sir Neville Bowman-Shaw. In 1990 Sir Neville was named as joint 167th richest man in Britain by the Sunday Times.

Advert for the 1982 Toddington Show The first show was held in 1978 and was little more than a village fete and horse show. The show has grown and attained county status in 1983, when the name was changed to the South Beds County Show. The 40 acre showground at Herne Manor Farm is made available by Sir Neville and Lady Bowman-Shaw.

South Beds County Show, 1991. Pictured is Master Robert Hart, being supervised by a member of Dunstable Bowmen in the art of toxophily (archery). It is interesting to note that Henry VIII, Mary Queen of Scots and Elizabeth I all practised archery.

Toddington in 1892

Extracts from the Luton News in 1892:

7 January

COURSING. – On Boxing Day a coursing match was held in Mr Dean's meadows and was largely attended. About 60 rabbits were caught.

The Rev J. Cooper, who has been curate of the parish for four years, has left for Norfolk, where he has undertaken similar duties.

CHOIR TEA. – On Friday evening the young members of the choir of the parish church were entertained to tea at the Rectory, and a very enjoyable evening was afterwards spent.

STORM. – Toddington was visited by a hail and snow storm on Wednesday morning. Some of the inhabitants were much alarmed as they feared a similar storm to that of last October, when about a hundred windows were smashed.

TEA. – On Jan. 1st the annual teachers' tea was held at the Wesleyan schools, when the teachers and two first Bible classes attended. The annual social meeting followed, when several interesting addresses were given by the superintendents and secretary, and songs were sung.

MAGIC LANTERN. – Capt West, lecturer from the Royal Naval Exhibition, interested a large audience at the National schools on Friday, whilst he discoursed upon, 'The heavens, the earth, and under the sea.' The lecture was admirably illustrated by a powerful lantern, and at the conclusion a number of comic sketches were given, which afforded the audience considerable amusement.

CHRISTMAS TREE AND SOIREE. – A Christmas tree and soiré were held on Boxing Day at the Wesleyan schools. A good trade was done during the afternoon, and in the evening the school was crowded to hear a miscellaneous entertainment, consisting of songs, recitations, dialogues, etc, rendered by gentlemen and ladies of the neighbourhood. An interesting feature of the evening was a fifteen minutes' chat on electricity by Mr F. Ashby.

31 March

THE SOUP KITCHEN, which was opened at the end of January, was closed for the season on Thursday, more than a hundred quarts of soup having been distributed weekly during that time. The Rev A. Adams had a large copper set up at the Rectory for the making of the soup.

7 April

THE RESTORATION of the parish church is greatly prospering, Major Cooper Cooper, of Toddington Manor, having consented to repair the stone work of the south transept, and Miss Cooper Cooper has promised to add to its adornment by the gift of a stained glass window to the memory of her mother. New items of interest in the history of Toddington are continually cropping up as the result of investigation. Not the least of these is the fact that the first Lord Russell, Earl of Bedford, married his bride from Toddington (see *Woburn and its Abbey,* London, 1890). She was the heiress of the Cheneys, and by this marriage the Dukes of Bedford became possessed of Chenies, the model village of Buckinghamshire (then spelt Cheneys), which has been their burial place ever since. There are three fine old altar tombs in the south transept to Lord Henry, Lady Jane and Lady Ann Cheney; but they are in a sadly dilapidated condition. It is of additional interest to be able to report that Flitcroft, the famous architect who re-built three if not four sides of the great quadrangle of Woburn Abbey, lies buried in Toddington churchyard.

5 May

THE JUVENILE FORESTERS. – On Monday evening a concert, arranged by Corporal T. N. Hughes, of Luton, and District Chief Ranger of the Luton District of the Ancient Order of Foresters, was given in the National schools, on behalf of the Juvenile Foresters Friendly Society, by members of the Luton Volunteer Detachment and others, Sergeant F. Pitkin being MC. The Rev F. A. Adams occupied the chair and was supported by Councillor Dillingham, Col-Sergt Gething, Sergt Hargraves, Sergt F. Scott and Sergt Goffing. The Chairman, in opening the entertainment, remarked that the object before them was one of the noblest and best, and he urged all parents who had not yet entered their boys in the club to do so at once. Sickness would come to all at some time or other and it was well to be prepared for it, and if it never came they would have the satisfaction of knowing they had helped some others who had been less fortunate in this respect. He impressed upon those present the necessity of keeping their contributions regularly paid as it was most distressing and disheartening to a minister on going to the sick bed, to find people unprovided for and that they had contributed to a Friendly Society for years but had allowed their contributions to lapse.

12 May

AN EXTRAORDINARY RUMOUR. – Quite a commotion was caused in Toddington on Saturday evening, about nine o'clock, owing to the rumour that a young man well known in the district had been found hanging in the Chalton Spinneys. This person was apprenticed to a tradesman at Toddington some years ago, but had subsequently got into difficulties, and was in the town on Saturday, asking for alms from some whom he had previously known. How the rumour got about that he had taken his life is not known, for the police, on making investigations, found there was no foundation whatever in the story.

12 May

THE NATIONAL SCHOOL. – The distribution of prizes took place at the National school on Friday afternoon, by the Rev F. A. Adams. Books to the number of 131 were distributed among the infants and in the mixed department prizes were given to each child who had made 400 attendances out of a possible 430. Fifty-four boys and fifty-four girls obtained the awards. In addition to the attendance prizes in each standard, merit prizes were given; these were for punctuality, cleanliness, attention, and progress. In Standard I, nine prizes were given, Margaret Thomas being first; and in Standards II to VII, the first prizes were awarded respectively to Wilfrid Joy, Harry Timms, Horace Briden, Emily Timms, Charles Thomas and Sarah J. Briden. The latter also received a very handsome writing case for acting as sewing monitor. The pupil teachers and assistants likewise received small gifts.

26 May

AN UNLICENSED DOG. – At the Woburn Petty Sessions, Frank Boston, baker, of Toddington, was summoned for keeping a dog without a licence, and was fined 2s 6d, and 13s 2d costs.

A CART ON FIRE. – On Saturday afternoon, between four and five o'clock, Mr Anthony Fossey, market gardener, of Toddington, was returning from Luton Market with his horse and a cart load of hampers. When nearing the Luton Laundry, on the Dunstable-road, he heard an alarm of fire, and, looking behind him, to his amazement he discovered the hampers at the back of the cart were on fire. He had in the front part of the cart with him the manager of the Luton Laundry, and three children, who were immediately lifted from the cart and the horse detached. Means were at once resorted to extinguish the fire, which now had got a good hold of the hampers, and were blazing away furiously. Some men at the Laundry seeing the fire at once set to work filling a barrel of water, and hastened to the scene, but their efforts were in vain, the whole of the hampers being burned and the body of the cart, leaving only the wheels and iron work. The cart was a borrowed one, it having been lent to Mr Fossey by his uncle, Mr Whitbread, carrier, of Toddington, while his own was undergoing repair. The estimated damage to the cart is six guineas and to contents £1. 14s, Both Mr Fossey and Mr Whitbread are insured with the Commercial Union Fire Office.

2 June

'OAK APPLE' DAY. – Sunday last being oak apple day, the bells of the parish church, in accordance with an old custom, were rung between the hours of three and five am, and boughs of oak were left at the doors of many of the inhabitants.

9 June

PITCH-AND-TOSS. – At the Woburn Petty Sessions, on Friday, Edward Clarke, Joseph Coles, William Kingham, George Hide, Samuel Hide, and Thomas Garner, labouring lads, were charged with playing pitch-and-toss on a public footpath, leading from Harlington-road to Long-lane, at Toddington, on May 15th. Defendants pleaded guilty, and were fined 2s 6d and 6d costs each.

23 June

TEA TO WIDOWS AND ELDERLY WOMEN. – On Thursday Miss Caroline Cooper Cooper gave her summer tea to all the widows and elderly single women in the parish. Those who, through age or ill health, were unable to attend, were not forgotten, large supplies of the good things provided being sent to them. After tea, Messrs E.J.and F.E. Horley entertained the company with violin music, and all present took part in singing. Supper was served early, and then each guest received a small present, and left the School Loft, where the tea was given, well pleased with their afternoon and evening.

30 June

GENEROUS TREATMENT. – It will be fresh in the minds of our readers that a fire recently occurred on the highway, and a cart and a large number of garden hampers were consumed. The cart had been borrowed by a man named Fossy from W. Whitbread, and though both were insured in the Commercial Union Company, they were officially informed that no claim to compensation could be entertained, as the policy only covered the goods while on their premises. However, as both sufferers are working men, the Rev G. A. Adams took up their case, and, on his appeal, the company generously forwarded, through their agent, Mr G. Ellis, of High-street, a gratuity of £4 to be divided between them.

4 August

DRUNKENNESS. – At the Woburn Petty Sessions on Friday, Edward Harris, labourer, of Toddington, was charged with having been drunk and disorderly on the highway at that place on the 12th July. He was fined £1 and 7s 6d costs. Charles Buckingham and Charles Fleckney, labourers, of Toddington, charged with a similar offence, were fined £1 and 7s 6d costs each.

ASSAULTING A POLICE-CONSTABLE. – At the Woburn Petty Sessions on Friday, John Hack, labourer of Toddington, was charged with having assaulted Pc Mears, while the latter was in the execution of his duty, on the 9th July, and he was convicted and fined 5s and 7s 6d costs.

THE RESTORATION OF THE PARISH CHURCH. – In order to help swell the fund being raised to carry out the above work, a tea, followed by games and a promenade concert, was held last Thursday afternoon in the grounds attached to the Rectory. There was a goodly gathering, and after tea different games were enjoyed until half-past six, when Miss Twydel opened the concert with a piano solo. This lady, in conjunction with Miss Browning, acted as accompanist during the evening. The programme consisted of glees, by the choir; quartettes and solos, by Miss Noblet and Mr Dowse; Misses Sarah J. Briden and Minnie Smith, and Master Chas. G. Thomas, depicted a scene from Dick Whittington; and the 'Old Maids of Lea' brought the first part of the programme to a close. The get-up of the old maids evoked roars of laughter. The second part had to be given up, owing to the intense coldness of the air, and the visitors amused themselves with games. At a quarter to nine the National Anthem was sung, and cheers for the Rev F. A. Adams were given. The gathering was a success.

AN EXTRA GUARDIAN FOR TODDINGTON. – At the Easter vestry meeting a resolution was passed that it was desirable to memorialise the Local Government Board to appoint a third guardian for the parish, and it was shown that Toddington's rateable value was very much larger than any other parish in the Union. The result has been that the warrant was received last week to appoint a new guardian before the 20th of the present month, and the ratepayers have begun to look about them for eligible candidates. Several gentlemen seem anxious for the office, but it was thought by a large number of the inhabitants that it was desirable to secure a working-man candidate – one who had known the struggle of life and seen both sides of it, and accordingly, on Saturday, a deputation waited upon Mr Samuel Walters, market gardener, of Toddington. The matter was laid before him, and he consented to stand, expressing his determination to fight the people's battle, and if elected to attend the Board and do his duty. Regardless of smiles or frowns, when this decision became known, the working men of the parish at once commenced a vigorous canvass, and Mr Walters's return seems pretty sure. Mr Samuel Walters is a man about 70 years of age, although he looks much younger. He is very healthy and robust, and in fact, is the Grand Old Man of Toddington. In his younger days he knew the 'pinch', having lived through the time of the Crimea when bread was a shilling a loaf, and other provisions equally dear, and having to work then for a few shillings a week to support a small family (or a large one) of small children. But by dint of industry, hard at it and always at it, he had brought his children up respectably, with great credit to himself. At the present time he and his sons are working a large market gardening business. He is a man well read, with a good grasp of the land question, and he has studied for years the system of the poor law. He is, in fact, a thorough-going intelligent Radical, and if a contest is not avoided it is quite certain that at the poll Mr Walters will have the unanimous vote of the working men of the parish. Many of the inhabitants are looking forward to the contest with keen interest.

11 August

GUN ACCIDENT. – On Monday morning, as Mr A. Horley's son was out in the garden field with his father's gun for the purpose of scaring away birds from the fruit, he shot at a rising bird, not knowing that about forty yards off, in the next garden, a number of children were fruit gathering. Unfortunately three of the youngsters were injured by the shots. Two of them, boys from London, were not seriously hurt, although very much frightened, but the other, a lad named Hide, who was on a visit to his uncle, received about twenty shots in different parts of the body. At first it was thought that the injuries were of a very grave character, but upon examination, the doctor, who was immediately sent for, found the boy was only suffering from flesh wounds. There was considerable loss of blood, but the lad is now progressing favourably.

18 August

TENT MISSION. – Mr Whiting of the Evangelistic Society, London, commenced a mission at Toddington, on Monday, in a large tent erected in Mr A. R. Skelton's field, on the Leighton-road. The services are quite unsectarian, and a choir has been formed from the choirs of the various places of worship to assist with the services. The mission is to last a month.

25 August

TENT MISSION. – The services in connection with the above, so far have been most successful. On Sunday, the tent, which holds nearly 500 people, was crowded at both services, and the collections have been good. Mr Whiting, the missioner, is a man who takes the people well; his addresses are plain, pointed, earnest, and full of good illustrations and incidents from his own experience and calculated to do much good. As the mission progresses, the interest seems to deepen.

1 September

TENT MISSION. – On Tuesday, a strong gale was blowing and unfortunately, the canvas of the mission tent was rent, and the cords breaking, the tent was blown over and damaged so that it cannot be put up again until it is thoroughly repaired. The managers of the Wesleyan day-schools have unanimously offered Mr Whiting, the evangelist, their school to hold his mission services for the next fortnight.

BRAVE RESCUE FROM DROWNING. – On Friday, while several boys were fishing in the Town Pond, a boy from London fell over the edge of the pond into a part where it is more than six feet deep and went under twice. A lad named Athews at once plunged in to his rescue and caught hold of his hand just in time to save him from going down the last time, but as he was out of his depth, he would have sunk with his charge had not his mother run to his rescue and taking hold of his hand dragged both to the edge of the water where they were rescued. After a time the boy came round and is now almost recovered from the immersion. A correspondent writes to know whether it is not [time] a fence was put round the most dangerous part of this pond before any lives are lost.

22 September

CONDEMNED WATER. – . . . . a letter was read from the solicitors of Mrs Tearle, of Toddington, requesting the Board to inform her what analyst should be engaged to test the water in a well upon her property, condemned by the Sanitary officers. The well had since been cleaned out but the Board required the report of an analyst. The Chairman considered it was not the business of the Board to specify any particular analyst.

6 October

RECREATIVE EVENINGS. – The head master, Mr R. Pearce, of the Wesleyan schools is taking a new departure this year. On Tuesday he commenced an evening class for young men which is to be held three evenings a week, at the small fee of one penny. There is to be an hour's instruction, and the rest of the time is to be taken up with reading and games, daily papers being provided and about 400 books, periodicals and magazines. On Tuesday evening 15 lads availed themselves of the opportunity and it is expected a large number will attend. Prizes will be given at the close of the session to those who have attended regularly and passed the examination in March.

THE ELECTION. – On Thursday the polling for this district went on quietly. One great drawback was the lack of vehicles on the Liberal side and towards evening as the rain came down in torrents it was found impossible to bring up every voter; but on the whole they came up well. On Friday both parties waited anxiously for a telegram announcing the result, as several of the Liberals had gone to Luton to hear the poll declared. About one o'clock a telegram was received which made it appear that Duke was in by 242, and the Tories were naturally very jubilant, but they were not so well pleased when it afterwards transpired that the 242 was on the other side.

13 October

THE REV F. A. ADAMS ON THE PROSPECTS OF THE COMING WINTER. – Preaching at All Saints' Church Leighton, last week, the occasion being the harvest festival, the Rev F. A. Adams, rector of Toddington, said it was the duty of the preacher on such an occasion, whoever he might be, to make an earnest appeal to the people to express their gratitude to the Almighty for the mercies of the year, and, whereas those in the villages had much to be grateful for, it was still easier to make that appeal to those who lived in the towns, as being the more prosperous of the two. The position of those who lived in the country he said, was becoming unmistakably very serious. The hay crop was very light; wheat was this year a comparative failure; and he was assured by employers that, with prices as low as they were, it was likely to be a hard winter for the poor. There was a grave probability of many finding themselves out of work, and that the wages of the remainder would sink. Last winter wages had only been eleven shillings a week round Toddington, and they might come down to ten. He had no hesitation in saying that things in the country called for the most serious consideration of the legislators. The laws which had been designed for the general good, having no limit to their operation, were beginning to prove a curse instead of a blessing.It really seemed to him that they were being gradually starved out of their own land. In many respects improvement must be admitted, but many in the congregation could remember when the poor could make fifteen shillings a week by plaiting, whereas it was now a matter of difficulty to earn half-a-crown, and wages which might have been fourteen and fifteen shillings a week were in Bedfordshire only eleven, and might yet be only ten. He quite failed to see the advantages the poor enjoyed which quite compensated for this great loss in the reward of their labour.The condition of the village industries certainly called for attention and redress, and he said this from a great sense of duty and responsiblity. At the same time they realised that on every hand they had much for which to be sincerely grateful – not only for what was gathered from the fields, but for a thousand other mercies.

27 October

A CIRCULATING LIBRARY in connection with the Wesleyan Schools, has been inaugurated by Miss M. A. Roberts and a small committee of young ladies, for the circulation of purely moral and religious literature. Sufficient money has been collected for the purchase of about sixty books, and with this number a start has been made. Other volumes will be added as contributions and donations come in. It is felt that this will supply a long-felt want, in connection with the education and moral elevation of the large number of young people who are connected with the church.

10 November

THE 'FIFTH'. – There was no demonstration here on the 'fifth.' In previous years there has always been a large bonfire on the green but no one seemed to take any interest in the matter, and beyond a few boys dressed as guys, there was nothing to commemorate the gun powder plot.

GAME TRESPASS. – At the Woburn Petty Sessions last Friday, before Mr O. P. Stuart and Major Downes, Joseph Brandon, labourer, of Toddington, was charged with a game trespass on land in the occupation of Thomas William Holmes, at Toddington, on October 21st. The case having been gone into, a fine of 5s with 10s 6d costs, or 14 days' hard labour, was inflicted.

17 November

SANITARY. – Special complaint was made at the Woburn Sanitary meeting, on Friday, by Mr Attwood, sanitary inspector, in regard to two contaminated wells at Toddington and nuisance arising from a discharging closet pit in connection with four cottages at Ridgmont. The latter case and one of the wells had been reported upon some months back, and notices had been served upon the owners, but without result. The Board directed that final notices be served upon the owners to close the wells, the water of which was said to be past verification; and it was further stated that water for consumption was obtained by the occupiers of the properties from the town pump. A final notice was also directed to be served in reference to the Ridgmont case.

25 November

A BOON FOR THE OLD FOLKS. – Mrs Murray Smith and the Misses Hicks have taken in hand the needs and comfort of the aged poor of the parish for years past. Every Wednesday afternoon a large number of poor old people in receipt of parish relief have had to stand outside the Griffin Inn or in the yard, waiting to receive their doles from the relieving officer who distributes them to the various recipients in the above yard. These ladies have now made arrangements for the old malthouse at the Griffin to be placed at their disposal; a good fire is to be provided every Wednesday afternoon, and seats, so that the old people, some of whom have to walk two miles to take their relief, shall have a little comfort while they have to wait.

15 December

TECHNICAL INSTRUCTION. – Mr Frank Spooner, BA, organising secretary to the County Council, gave his lecture on 'a grain of wheat,' at the National School, Toddington, on Thursday evening. The room was well filled.

22 December

THE CEMETERY. – The Burial Board have been busy lately in trying to effect a great improvement in this rather desolate-looking graveyard. It is splendidly situated, commanding most extensive and beautiful views, but in itself has hitherto been bare and cheerless. During the past week more than fifty trees and shrubs from Messrs Lane's nurseries have been carefully planted, and should they do well they will effect a great change for the better in the appearance of the cemetery.

29 December

THE CHURCH. – On Christmas day sermons suitable to the season were preached by the Rev F. A. Adams. The church was tastefully decorated for the occasion and the anthems were ably rendered by the choir; Mr C.E.Thomas presiding at the organ. There were good congregations at all the services, which were fully choral.

COALS TO THE POOR. – This year the usual dole of coals to the poor of the parish have not been given for some unaccountable reason, and a good deal of disappointment is felt by the usual recipients. Many of the very poor feel keenly the pinch of the very cold weather which has set in upon us, and it is hoped the needs of these deserving poor will not be overlooked.

WESLEYAN CHAPEL. – A Christmas tree and sale of useful and fancy articles was held in the schoolroom on Boxing day. Tea and refreshments were provided at moderate charges, and vocal and instrumental music was rendered by the newly formed Sunday school choir, under the leadership of Mr A. Neale. Various amusements were provided, and a pleasant social evening was spent. An interesting and instructive feature of the evening's entertainment was a lecture on electricity, illustrated by experiments by Mr A. J. Ashby of the firm of John Davis & Sons, Derby. The schoolroom was crowded, and the proceeds for the chapel and schools were considered satisfactory.

Toddington Memories

Extract from *Toddington Memories* by R.V.H. Seymour recalling life in the early part of this century:

Sunday was a special day, with special clothes to wear, special food to eat and special behaviour. A lot that was right on weekdays was wrong on Sundays. Only essential work had to be done, the milkman came in the morning, with his two cans hanging from a yoke across his shoulders, his half pint measure hooked inside the can. A man came round pushing a soap box on wheels, with newspapers in it, but the observers of the Sabbath did not accept this as essential, regarding the selling as akin to wickedness, and would not read or buy them. There was plenty of time in the week, they said, to read about the evil goings-on in the world without reading about it on Sundays. The cowman made two journeys to the farm to feed and milk his cows, returning home for two or three hours in the middle of the day to enjoy a cooked midday meal and afterwards a quiet pint, as did the horsekeeper attending his horses. Rarely, in health, did either of them have a whole day off. There were those also who, having time on their hands, did nothing, or drifted to the pub for a drink while some gave their wife a helping hand by preparing the meal. On summer evenings, the less enthusiastic churchgoers would take the children for long country walks, which they much preferred to attending the services. Nevertheless the attendance of church or chapel for the observance of the Sabbath was the accepted custom for many of the inhabitants, only differing perhaps in one respect from that of the late Victorians, namely the defiant refusal of some of the labourers to accept church or chapel attendance as an unwritten condition of their job, although often like attracted like when the businessman or shopkeeper engaged an assistant.

My parents decided that I should become a Wesleyan and at an early age, dressed up and ready, I was collected from home by young lady Sunday school teachers, but soon became independent and made my own way. The services were Sunday school 9.30-10.20 am, chapel 10.30-12 noon, Sunday school 2.00-3.00 pm, chapel 6.00-7.30 pm. Sunday school was held in the same school as for weekdays and the chapel was in the High Street, so at the end of the morning school we were lined up in pairs and then marched to the chapel, teachers at regular intervals along the side of the column and one behind to see that no one strayed. A number of menfolk also gave their time, and occupied the more responsible school positions such as secretary, to mark the register (this was important, as there were a number of rewards for regular attendance), and superintendent, who was in charge. Men also taught the senior classes, although when I was in the senior boys' class, a lady by the name of Mrs Vidler took it. She walked the mile and a half from Herne Manor Farm for the afternoon services, and her sincerity and kindliness acquired such an authority that I can remember no incident of disrespect or bad behaviour while she was there.

The school room was parted from the school house by a thin wall and on some occasions the noise became so great that the schoolmaster, being disturbed, appeared at the school room door, wearing that most forbidding look. We were glad that it was not a school day, and both officals and scholars were for a time somewhat subdued. Although he held various chapel offices he drew the line at taking Sunday School classes, but sometimes found himself called upon to fill in for an absent teacher and was known to get out of his chair and fireside slippers in a rather grudging manner.

At chapel we sat in the gallery, girls on one side, boys on the other. The preacher generally relieved the morning's tedium with a story for the children and should we get fidgety there were scowls and fierce looks from elderly gentlemen who, we were convinced, did not approve of children at all. Afternoon school was reasonably pleasant. We were dismissed early enough to make a detour home through the fields and provided we refrained from getting ourselves too muddy, or being seen by prying eyes, we would relieve our pent-up feelings.

The Sunday school anniversary services were held on Easter Sunday and were the most important services of the year. They were all held in the chapel. The children had been learning special anniversary hymns for some weeks before, and the choir had been busy with their anthems. A special preacher, adjudged to be popular, was engaged. On Sunday afternoon the service was for children, when they received prizes for attendance and good behaviour, the latter being in some cases very much assumed. Parents were welcomed to watch their proud offspring receive their books and could bring younger children and babies, when no notice was taken if they decided to contribute their own sound effects. Sometimes, however, they would exceed the limit with a loud and unstoppable howl, and were taken outside by their flustered mother, only to stop immediately they were outside the door. After a little while the mother, greatly daring, would return, just in time we hope, to hear her older offspring sing a verse of 'Jesus Wants Me for a Sunbeam'.

At the evening service the choir took over with anthems and solos. The chapel was packed, many coming from the surrounding villages, and mighty indeed was the singing of 'Christ the Lord Is Risen Today'. The great sound was again repeated at the Harvest Festival, when congregations again filled the chapel to capacity, only now it was 'We Plough the Fields and Scatter'. Every possible nook was decorated with country produce, sheaves of corn, loaves of bread, vegetables, garlands of rose hips, and always a great pumpkin. The atmosphere was one of friendliness and affability, and the meeting of old friends. The austerity, so much a part of Methodism at that time, was just a little relaxed.

The church, too, had its festivals on customary occasions, the singing perhaps a little less robust than the Methodists', as would befit its status, but of equal importance to those concerned with it. I know of no shopkeeper and few businessmen who were not involved with one denomination or the other, and since their influenuce affected, directly or indirectly, nearly everyone else in the town, these occasions were anticipated with great interest socially as well as religiously.

The pressures of war, however, were to bring about many changes that would cause old customs to break up. I had reached teenage and was approaching adolescence, at a time when nothing was sure or secure. Sunday became much of a vacuum. I think some of my first thoughts of uncertainty were caused by those Harvest Festivals just described. There seemed to me a certain illogicality about some of their assumptions. The singing of the hymn,

> 'All things bright and beautiful,
> All creatures great and small,
> All things wise and wonderful,
> The Lord God made them all.'

when followed by a prayer thanking the Lord for the bread and meat put on their table, aroused in me some scepticism. I became critical of the dogmas that up to now had affected my upbringing. The instability of the new times was having its effect on things that hitherto had been regarded as permanent. New ways of spending Sunday were found, and the disapproving looks from an older generation were ignored. A number of us still attended one or the other of the religious services in the evening partly from habit, partly for something to do, and in my case at least from an enjoyment of singing and music, and there was still time for teenage groups to get together and roam the fields in the summer evening.

When the evenings were long and the weather fine, the appeal of the countryside was irresistible, and the congregations became a little thinned as one or both parents decided to take their restless offspring for a walk. Those that had been to the services and had no children to cope with took a short stroll afterwards, enjoying leisurely conversation as they went, habitually turning back at certain accepted points: the Park drive in Milton Road, the Mile Stile in Leighton Road, Chalgrave Turn, or Lords Hill in Dunstable Road. Traffic was almost non-existent, and groups of twos or threes would walk at intervals along the centre of the road, disturbed only perhaps by Farmer Attwood trotting home from church in his governess cart or Mr George Scrivner, home from the Baptist chapel in his. With a wave of the whip in passing, and a cheery 'Good night' to those they knew, and they knew them all, the clip clop of the pony's hoofs speeded up for a moment or two, then it was peace again, except for the sound of conversation and laughter that was carried on the air.

Tired children returning from the woods, dropping flowers that they had been so excited to pick, were passed by dawdling couples, absorbed by a silent interest in each other's company. This was the pleasant face of those days, made easier to remember by the long sunlit evenings, the green fields, and the flowers on the hedges. In this I was lucky; I had an uncle who was one of a school of countrymen, now alas no more, who knew every fieldpath, every pond, the call of each bird and where it nested, why this field had been ploughed in this manner and the other in that. He was mild and informative by nature and walked the fields alone, or welcomed the company of children or visitors. When I was old enough to join him on these rambles, my parents found life much more peaceful if I was with him, rather than enduring the tedium of a sermon, and so a seed was sown. I learned that things, as well as men, were equal, and had their place under the sun, and that nowhere was this more true than in the country.

It must have rained sometimes, and there was of course, winter as well as summer, no television or radio, only a gramophone with a horn, that few could afford to possess. People provided their own music. The most popular instrument was the piano, and it was surprising how many people contrived to possess one. The earlier ones had a front panel of fretwork, with red silk shining through, on to which were fixed two hinged brass candlesticks, the whole being a veritable dust trap. Earlier still was the cottage organ, worked by wind, blown from a creaking foot treadle, and with even more ornamental fretwork. The sound of one of these coming through the wall of our cottage, when played by our self-taught neighbour, was most impressive. Her rendering of 'Rescue the Perishing' from the Shanky and Moody Hymnal, being very sobering. Then came the day of the sentimental ballad, composed by people like F.E. Weatherly, and Stephen Adams. Anyone with a bass or tenor voice could always find a welcome, it was surprising how quickly half a dozen people would be gathered round the piano when the singing started.

The radio, known then as a wireless, had by 1920 found its way into the homes of a few enthusiasts and experimenters. The first time I heard it was on a Sunday evening at Coelwulf, the home of Mr Harry Fletcher, in Park Road. The set was a crystal set, and we wore headphones to hear a performance of *The Messiah*. It was the first time that I had heard the work and despite the sound occasionally vanishing, and the crystal needing at times to be tickled, its majesty could not be denied and I learned a new dimension in music. The performance was helped along by our host who knew it well and had a tenor voice, being particularly strong in the *Hallelujah Chorus*.

Schooldays in the 1930s

Life in the 1930s as seen through the eyes of Priscilla Hart:

I started at the National school in Station Road in 1930. My first teacher at school was Miss Annie Walker, and I can still remember clearly the wooden frame on a stand at the front of the class on which we learnt to weave by passing a stick through the bands of braid. The next class was taken by Miss Dolemore (Mrs Pett). Here I remember copying letters of the alphabet in pencil and the joy of receiving a present from Father Christmas after the school play – it was a table-tennis set. Next came Miss Flora Seymour (Mrs Nelsey) and here there was great competition to get your sums right. Every Friday afternoon she produced a sweet tin and each pupil who had done well, chose his or her favourite humbug. Miss Garratt (Mrs Briden) later took over this class and then followed Miss Elizabeth Higgs, famous for her history lessons. My final teacher was Miss Ashcroft (Mrs Joy). In this class Miss Ashcroft really made us work and every year some pupils passed the entrance exams for the High, Modern and Technical Schools in Luton. She was excellent with a sewing needle and taught us girls to hem, darn and embroider. Hard words to spell were remembered by rhymes or song e.g. Mrs D, Mrs I, Mrs F F I, Mrs C, Mrs U, Mrs L T Y-Difficulty. On Friday afternoon we had the treat of a story, when she read aloud *A Christmas Carol*, *Kidnapped* and *The Water Babies,* etc. Many a tear was shed and a smile made as her voice altered for each character, making the book come alive.

Mr Bruce Wootton was headmaster and taught the top class. He was good at handling the senior boys, and was keen on music and gardening. A curtain divided his class from Miss Higgs' and many a time a splash of ink was thrown from an ink pen onto this curtain in the hope of hitting a pupil in the lower class. Inkwells were filled up each morning by pupils who also brought coke into school from the coal shed for the school stoves.

As I lived a mile away from school, I was allowed to stay to school lunch. These were cooked and served on the premises of the Council School and eaten in the school hall. The chief cook was Mrs Crawley and later Mrs Crump and they will long be remembered for their treacle puddings with custard and spotted dicks. Every girl having a dinner took turns in helping to prepare the vegetables and wash up afterwards. A few lessons were missed in the peeling of potatoes, etc, and time lost in the dinner hour while washing up – the boys were not expected to do these chores!

In the early 1930s I used to bus to school in winter (1d fare from Fancott Bridleway near the letter box to Toddington Green) and walk on the fine summer days. In the spring we used to count the number of dead frogs lying in the road from the Fancott claypits to the hill – sometimes it came to over 100. They had all been run over and squashed flat! Another game was to walk the first two telegraph poles and then run the next. When I received a pair of roller skates these were also used to skate the mile to school and provided amusement in the playground as well.

School sports were held in Mr Ayres' field next to the school playground. We were allocated four Houses as teams – Red (St George), Yellow (St David), Green (St Patrick), and Blue (St Andrew). I remember great excitement one day when Johnny Kempton jumped higher than himself. Extra holidays were always enjoyed – especially Pancake Day on Shrove Tuesday, when the older children were allowed out of school at 11.50 am to run over to Conger Hill. When the pancake bell tolled midday, we listened to the old woman frying her pancakes and really believed we could hear the sizzling. Empire Day (24 May) and Ascension Day were also half day holidays. With the latter it was a service in church and then the older children were allowed to go up the church tower.

For various reasons some children could not attend school. Mr Cross, the education attendance officer, would often appear on parents' doorsteps to know the reason why. His name only had to be mentioned in Toddington and some parents and pupils would tremble – such was the fear of the man! The school dentist used to visit schools about once a year and he and his nurse used to take over a small classroom for his visit. None of us liked his treatment, of course, and another dislike was the nurse who looked into your hair for nits.

My pocket money was usually 1d per week, but often I would meet my father in the school lunch break, have a short ride in the milk float and talk him into giving me another penny to spend. Numerous shops and pubs sold sweets in Toddington, but my favourites were the ones I passed on my way to school. Cliffords, the bakery, was where one of my friends, Edna, lived with her sister Ann. Another favourite not far from Timms was Mrs Capell at the *Nag's Head*. My father often called here, so being friends I was a back-door customer and she always gave me good value for my penny.

Village Inns

The following article by Page Woodcock appeared in the *Bedfordshire Magazine*, Autumn 1949:

The earliest 'hangover' experienced at Toddington is not on record, but throughout the ages the town has seen much to celebrate, and it is pleasant to picture in imagination the imbibing of those folk of early days who had the wherewithal.

Tuda, the Saxon, names for us the Totingedune or Dodintone of the Domesday Book of 1086, a document which introduced the civil service to Toddington and the compiling of which must have been very thirsty work. William the Conqueror gifted Toddington to one Ernulfus de Hesdin. Ernulfus's widowed daughter, in turn, gifted the church to Toddington, and it is pleasant again to reflect on the amount of ale and French wine those early builders must have quaffed. Dry work in any age, stone-masonry.

Inns, the public-houses of today have always been a fair barometer of the spending power of the people. Private enterprise in the person of Paulinus Peyvre, a man of 'mean origin', one-time steward to the court of Henry III, brought prosperity to Toddington by building his manor there, and during his occupation the first market grant was given to the town by a royal warrant of 1218. 'Mean origin' or not, Paulinus is recorded as having paid his workmen and builders generously. Seven hundred years ago, at his instigation, and to cater for his employees with their pleasantly chinking purses, the forerunners of today's inns began to cluster around the village green and the new church. Paulinus died in 1251, doubtless proud of his achievements as a self-made man.

The Thursday market was changed to Saturday under Edward II, becoming one of the largest in the county, and by 1377, when the population was 600, inns abounded and taverns increased their accommodation for the ever-growing numbers of traders and travellers.

Grotesques around a Church
I created quite a controversy when I visited Toddington recently to find out which was its most ancient inn. At the *Sow and Pigs* I found my first 'local' authorities, mostly pint-tankard-sized men, headed by Mr J. Hanson, the proprietor. Pryce Jones, my companion on this fact-finding tour, assured me that the inn obtained its sign from the frieze of sows and pigs on the old Gothic church opposite. Soberly viewing the greatly weathered cornice chiselled in Totternhoe stone, I was startled to see that one 'sow' possessed what looked like the hind legs of a kangaroo. Closer inspection revealed even more unnatural members of the pig family until I became convinced that the bucolic masons who carved the animals had spent a considerable time in the inn itself. Joseph Hight Blundell's *Toddington* reassured me by listing in the frieze: 'two fishes with men's heads, a demi-man, a greyhound, a fox, a pair of peacocks, a mermaid, a chained leopard, a griffin, a cat, a chained lion with two bodies, twins, a rhinoceros, a demi-woman, a swan and a wyvern.' The Lysons call them 'grotesque' in their history, and 'grotesque' is the right word! We will absolve the *Sow and Pigs* inn, which may have been there before the cornice was carved, but I cannot help feeling that there is a distinct atmosphere of 'pink elephants' about the frieze.

Yet wyvern, swan and lion all figure in the arms of the family of Sir Thomas Cheney, to whom after various marriages the Peyvre manor descended. Sir Tom was Lord Warden of the Cinque Ports, which meant something in those days. In 1563, Queen Elizabeth visited Toddington (a great occasion for drinking!), stayed at the Cheneys' manor house and knighted the young son, Sir Henry. What a traffic jam there must have been in the town that day, with the Queen herself setting the new fashion of riding in a carriage, stableyards packed with horsemen and travellers, John Countryman and his family come from miles around to see the quality and the sights, all the quacks, thieves, charlatans and rogues ready to make a profit out of him, and taverns and ale-houses swamped with customers. From the 14th century it was the custom, because of the number of 'rough-houses', to impose a curfew on inns and taverns, a kind of predecessor of 'Time, gentlemen, please!' But on that day in 1563 in Toddington, extensions and 'sold out' notices were more likely.

The present *Sow and Pigs* was built about 1850, after its predecessor's demolition. Blundell says that the old house was 300 years old; certainly it was there in 1681, when '16 butchers alone had stalls on the market' and cluttered the green along with the market house, the maypole, the cattle pound and the blacksmith's forge. Gone is the market house which stood between today's Town Hall and the parish pump. It was demolished in 1799. Gone, too, is the maypole. What remains of the old pound lies alongside the smithy, which is now a petrol-filling station. Change, indeed!

With Pryce Jones, I developed great enthusiasm for inn research – during opening time – and occasionally we regretted the old days when Toddington could cater more fully for such tastes; when the Ram stood back of the smithy, the *White Horse* was reflected in the pond, when the *Queen's Head* and the *Wagon and Horses* (now a private house facing the green) still sold good ale; when you could drink at the *Star,* or the *Pheasant* (closed in 1920), or at the *Hare,* whose title was very likely a corruption of the now lost hamlet of Herne, nearby.

Alas, all these are gone. But the visitor still has a pretty choice with the *Sow and Pigs,* the *Nag's Head,* the *Bedford Arms,* the *Oddfellows Arms,* the *Bell,* the *Griffin,* the *Angel* and the *Red Lion.*

Before leaving the *Sow and Pigs,* we discovered that at the rear of this ancient site once stood the original parish workhouse; discovered also that in 1797 (the year of those cart-wheel twopences of George III) the Land Commissioners met there 'for a survey of all commons, homesteads, ancient enclosures, etc.' Then we were treated to a dissertation, by the local cronies, on that renowned sportsman and racehorse owner, 'Bob' Sievier. At the beginning of this century he not only raised, but also dashed the hopes of the neighbourhood with a horse named Sceptre. But he also organised some of the finest cricket that Toddington has ever seen; grand days, when the *Sow and Pigs* had always a huge ham in cut, and game-pie and sirloins of beef loaded the sideboard, ready to serve such famous people as W.G. Grace, Archie Maclaren and Tyldesley.

Gossip at the Griffin

Tearing ourselves away (Pryce Jones says that we lurched a little; but who can wonder?) we next visited the *Griffin.* Here, mine host Mr George Thomas made us welcome, but broke the sad news that the original *Griffin* was burnt out in 1904. This inn had great connections with the Earls of Strafford, the Wentworth family, on whose armorial bearing appears the griffin itself. No doubt it was flourishing on another great day for Toddington, when in 1608 James I arrived to stay at the manor. Undaunted by atrocious, unsurfaced, undrained roads, entirely without sign-posts or milestones, sight-seers and travellers once again poured into the town. Whilst royalty and nobility debated affairs of state at the manor, the 'regulars' chewed over the latest gossip in the bar-parlour of the *Griffin.*

Tragedy at the Manor

The choicest tit-bit of scandal they had had for many a long day was when the young and beautiful Henrietta, Baroness Wentworth, sheltered the Duke of Monmouth at the manor, which once stood in the 'Old Park'. An old plan shows that Henrietta and the Duke had adjoining rooms. Heigh-ho, what gossip! And – since the Duke, on the scaffold, is supposed to have declared his love and admitted that they had lived together as man and wife – with some substance to it. But gossip died when those same regulars saw, too, the death of poor Henrietta; of a broken heart, they avowed. Her mother erected for her an expensive tomb (it cost £2,000) in the church 263 years ago.

An occasion, this, for much mournful drinking, with the inn right next door to the church, a very convenient arrangement. Convenient indeed, for in 1725 it was being used as a meeting-place for parish affairs. Convivial gatherings they must have been; perhaps they grew too convivial, for the churchwardens' accounts for 1843 record that it was 'resolved with one dissentient voice' (bless him!) 'that the footpath leading from the church to the *Griffin Inn* be closed'.

Bad Days for Inn and Market
In 1853, when one Daniel Sheppard, victualler and farmer, kept the inn, an air of foreboding was introduced by the addition: 'also Inland Revenue Office'. But those were sad times when the local innkeeper had to have some other source of income or go out of business impoverished by the decline of the market. In 1864, Toddington still possessed eight inns and eleven beer retailers, and Thomas Gilbert, the carrier, left the *Sow and Pigs* twice a week for the *Rose Inn* at Smithfield, but the town was finding it increasingly difficult to compete with the markets of Dunstable and Luton and cope with the lack of rail facilties.

We left George Thomas in rather sombre mood, and briefly inspected the old Red Lion, now a private residence on the corner of the Ampthill Road. There we were joined by Mr William Brewer, a worthy gentleman whose family have lived in Toddington for generations. Once again revived the 'oldest pub' controversy. One of Mr Brewer's ancestors had kept the *Bell,* so we entered that house, and with the aid of the able proprietor, Mr W. B. Ayres, managed to sidestep another discussion on the sows and pigs on the church's frieze. Pryce Jones hedged very cleverly, and as we stood gazing through the low, broad bay-window at the village green, trying to picture the one-time Market House, brought the conversation back to the origin of this ancient inn.

As an inn-sign, bells in variations of one to eight seem to lie close to all churches. The *Bell* has been within the sound of others, apart from those of the Church In recent years the Town Bell was rung as a fire alarm and at one time the Market House bell was rung to open the weekly straw-plait market. And, talking of bells, in 1719 one Sir Henry Johnson, a rich ship-builder from Poplar, resided at the manor. Did the inn's sign originate from the ship's bell in compliment (as with the *Lion and Griffin*) to the lord of the manor?

The Bell Foundry
Our favourite theory goes back to 1412, when one 'William Rufford of Tudynton was belmaker'. Toddington's bell-foundry may well have been sited where the present inn stands, evolving itself eventually into a farm and then to an alehouse on either side of the present stable-yard entrance. The original licensed premises, by the way, stood on the left of the entrance. Most inns in Toddington move around once in a while, like the *Red Lion,* a pleasant house but licensed comparatively recently.

The 19th century saw great progress in coaching and with it, in innkeeping, but Toddington's languishing market more than outweighed the advantages of coaching. The *Sow and Pigs, Griffin* and *Bell* catered for passengers on the coaching routes from Bedford, Woburn and Ampthill, but slowly the traffic grew less, and travellers and visitors fewer. Many of the inns were forced to close, and those that remained fell sadly out of repair. Reflecting the general state of the town is the report that in 1813 the church windows were broken, its roof showed daylight, and the expensive tomb of dear Henrietta Wentworth lay damaged and dilapidated.

Until 1846, there was at least one thirsty customer visiting Toddington every day – the gentleman who arrived on horseback from Dunstable with the post. The town had no post office until that year.

In 1850, an attempt was made to revive the market again, but the new mode of travel, the railway, left Toddington high and dry. Its population decreased, whilst that of Luton grew fourfold, and Dunstable trebled in size. Craven's Directory of 1853 shows the innkeepers seeking additional work: 'William Horley, the *New Inn* (also shoemaker).' 'William Shaw, the *Sow and Pigs*, (also plumber and glazier).' Ann Baker was victualler at the *Bell* that year; and there were still nine beer retailers, Messrs. Allen, Bailey, Brewer, (that man again!), Cleavie, Fossey, Potts, Randall, Twidle and Wildman.

The advent of the motorist and improved roads, put Toddington back on the map again. In 1914 we find Henry Burridge at the *Bell* offering 'accommodation for motorists and cyclists' and – still the sideline – pedigree fox terriers. In that same year Bertie MacVicar Armstrong kept the *Sow and Pigs*, 'commercial and posting house', and one James Schleselman had the *Griffin*. According to some of our pint-sized local authorities this last-named suffered from the usual nonsensical spy-hunting.

'Frisky' earns his pint

Mr Brewer regaled us with several stories of the past. When, with Bombardier Billy Wells on the bill, Jim Fensome of Pitstone fought and beat Toddington's village policeman; of the times when the *Pheasant's* tankards all in use, men would drink out of their 'hard hats'. He remembered when 'a man could get bread, cheese, pickles, clay-pipe, baccy, a pinch of snuff, and enough beer to last him,' all for sixpence! When 'Frisky' Denton would come in the *Bell* and stand on his head while drinking a pint of beer, all for the price of the pint. Frisky indeed, for the old gentleman had seen eighty years!

Today, in spite of the dratted petrol rationing and the restriction of catering licences, one can still 'take one's ease at one's inn' in Toddington. Travel how you may, it is still worth while to wander into the cobbled yard of the *Sow and Pigs,* from where you can view that grotesque frieze opposite, or enter and inspect those racing accounts and caricatures of Bob Sievier's day. From the low-ceilinged bar of the *Bell,* peopled with the ghosts of good solid beer-drinking citizens, you can still gaze out on to the village green, the lay-out of which has remained unchanged for centuries.

There's something comforting about an old inn. What pleasanter company can you find than the 'regulars', what better conversation than chatting, tankard in hand, of old times?

Toddington in 1950

The following notes are based on a series of articles appearing in the *Toddington Parish News* which referred to a talk given by David Morgan to the Toddington Historical Society about village life in c1950:

I think we have witnessed a period of great change in the last 40 years. It has certainly not been the comparative plateau that was experienced during the 20 deflationary years between 1919 and 1939.

Toddington has not escaped; in fact, I would say our village has been too near the centre of the vortex for any escape to have been possible.

In 1950, when I first knew the village, milk was delivered by horse and cart and measured into jugs from silver churns. The doctor still did some of his rounds on horseback. The rector was still addressed as 'sir' and had been the incumbent for 25 years.

Education: The two all-range schools had only recently been altered by the 1944 Education Act; the National (Church) School becoming the Primary (5 to 11) and the Council School in Leighton Road becoming the Secondary Modern (11 to 15).

Prices: The return fare to Luton was 1/10d (8p approximately); and a pint of beer was a shilling (5p).

Wages: The average weekly wage of a farm worker was £6; the basic wage at Vauxhall was £10, the same applied to lorry drivers; assistant teachers were earning about £35 a month.

Shopping: Commercially Toddington was pretty well self-supporting. It sported a whole variety of shops: several general stores, a shoe shop, two clothiers, a couple of butchers and a fruiterer; fruit and veg. were sold in most of the general stores as was ironmongery and tobacco.

Transport: The motor was still a comparatively rare possession. There were two in Conger Lane (Gas Street); three, if you counted Dr Fawcett's ancient Austin 12.

House Purchase: I entered the village hoping to hear of a house for sale or to let; estate agents were pretty rare birds in those days and one kept one's ear to the ground. I heard of my house in the *Sow and Pigs* where I was lodging. Persuading Mr Candelent to let me buy it was a long, tedious and sometimes stormy business. Once the sale had been agreed, my relationship with Victor Seymour, whose firm was building it, began by my pestering the life out of him for a date when the property would be ready for occupation. This took a while in those days as all manufactured goods were in short supply or were on permit; the house had taken three and a half years to build because it had been built on six monthly quotas. Mr Seymour would use the materials allowed then go to another job to await the passing of another half year. However, we did move in on a cold Saturday in January 1951. My wife and baby daughter had spent the waiting period staying with my parents in South Wales. Victor and I are still the best of friends despite that early testing of our relationship.

Some Village Craftsmen: I used to haunt the house during this period of waiting and got to know the builders, especially Wilf Randall, a fine craftsman. A carpenter by trade, he could turn his hand to most crafts to do with building. He was also an excellent gardener and was the village authority on bee-keeping. He was a man of strong opinions and wasn't averse to telling you what he thought, even if he had to hurt you a little; but his deeds were extremely generous and I am still benefitting from his fine craftsmanship.

Another village craftsman was Chris Fleckney, electrician, motor mechanic, blacksmith and taxi driver. Chris was fond of his half pint and had a wide field-range. Many a man got tipsy looking for Chris as he was much in demand. He was a wit and very well read; no one knew when he did his reading but he did it and he didn't suffer fools gladly. His establishment was where Toddington Service Station now is and petrol was dispensed from a single hand-pump. It was usually self service because Chris was rarely there and Mrs Fleckney was severely crippled with arthritis and so, after helping yourself, you walked through Mr Deal's upholstery shop to pay for it or have it booked; your honesty was never doubted.

Mr Frank Deal was Chris Fleckney's father-in-law. He had served his time as a coach-builder in the early Vauxhall factory. His workshop adjoined the Fleckney residence. I can remember being shown an invalid chair he'd built to his own design; it wasn't a wheelchair – just a chair that could be adjusted by a series of levers. His son-in-law, with whom he was not on the best of terms, reckoned that the poor invalid would probably die of a heart attack trying to work the thing.

Local Knight: Sir Frederick Mander was Toddington's brightest luminary in 1950. He had recently bought Wainholm and had retired there from being General Secretary of the National Union of Teachers throughout the war years. The headquarters of the NUT during the war, in evacuation, had been at Toddington Manor in Gloucestershire. He'd been knighted in recognition of his services to education; he'd had a large hand in the framing of the 1944 Education Act. He was born in Luton and had taught there, finishing as a headmaster before becoming a full-time union official. In 1950 he was chairman of Bedfordshire Education Committee and later chairman of the County Council. He died in 1963 and Lady Mander the following year. They had a paraplegic son whom they had nursed for nearly 40 years and had never known a full night's sleep because he had to be attended to during the night. A home had to be found for him. Finance for this had always been planned but the son only survived his parents by a year or so.

In 1950 Bruce Wootton died; Dr Fawcett died the following year. The passing of these two institutional figures along with the death of the Rev Hunt at about the same time seemed to represent the end of an era, especially when looked at in retrospect. Col Fawcett had been an army surgeon and had come to Toddington at the end of the First World War when he retired from the army. Most of the village looked on him as a kindly physician but also as a 'toff' and addressed him as such. They called him 'sir' as they did the rector; at least the men did, many of whom had been in the forces.

It was my privilege to know Mr Wootton, albeit for but a few months. He'd come to Toddington as a qualified assistant teacher just after the First World War but took over as headmaster when his predecessor retired. Much was expected of the 'heads' of church schools between the wars. They were expected to set a good example all round; to be the rector's righthand man; to be in charge of the Boy Scouts; raise funds to maintain the fabric of the building and pay for teaching materials. And last, but certainly not least, to raise money towards his own salary. Mr Wootton did all this and more. He was village correspondent for the *Luton News* and the Sun Insurance Company. During the Second World War he was the Citizens' Advice Bureau. He never grumbled about his load but I am in no doubt that the effort, over such a long period, shortened his life; he died in harness, months before he was due to retire. He ran a happy school and was greatly respected by both staff and pupils; and his relationship with the head of the secondary modern, Mr Young, was excellent. I was once loaned to him to help with his last sports day; I shall never forget it, it was a complete romp much enjoyed by everybody and not a stopwatch in sight.

Education

The pattern of school organisation in Bedfordshire (except Luton) today is a comprehensive system of lower schools (5-9 years), middle schools (9-13 years) and upper schools (13-19 years). Pre-school education is arranged through nursery schools (3-5 years), 4+ units and nursery units. Special education needs are met through special schools and special units. Schools now have the option of running their own affairs with money direct from the Department for Education.

This is very different from the situation in 1963, when T.S. Lucking, Director of Education, wrote the following brief history of the Toddington schools in the official opening programme of Parkfields School:

The first known school in Toddington was 'kept' in the 'Church House', now known as the Town Hall, on the west side of the churchyard in 1652. References exist to two headmasters in the 18th century and to a Mr William Horley, who is described as schoolmaster, as late as 1851. About this time, however, a National Church Enquiry included no day school in Toddington. There were, however, 280 pupils in attendance at a Sunday school.

In 1854 two day schools were set up. One was a Church of England school, which continues at the present time as the Toddington (Church of England) Voluntary Controlled Primary School, using its original buildings and associated temporary accommodation. The other was a Wesleyan school endowed by the will of Cyrus Smith. In 1910 this Wesleyan school was absorbed by the new school for 200 children which the county council built on adjacent land in Leighton Road. Both the Voluntary and the County schools offered an elementary education for pupils up to the age of 14 years.

In 1947 the two schools were re-organised; the Voluntary school providing for children between the ages of five and eleven and the County school for children over the age of eleven years. In 1958 the county council submitted proposals to the Minister of Education for the erection of new buildings to replace those in Leighton Road which since 1947 had housed the secondary school serving Toddington and the villages of Chalton, Chalgrave, Eversholt, Harlington, Milton Bryan and Tingrith. The Minister gave his approval in 1959 to these proposals and the school, now renamed Parkfields School moved into its new buildings on 22 April, 1963. Proposals have been submitted to the Minister that the buildings in Leighton Road, at present being used for primary school purposes, should be modernised and extended to become the new home of the primary school.

By the provision of these new buildings for Parkfields School, the educational facilities for both pupils and staff have been greatly extended. For the first time, the school has a library (planned to house some 5,000 to 6,000 volumes), fully equipped science laboratories, rooms for domestic science, needlework and art, and a craft shop, all equipped for the development of courses to be taken by pupils up to the Ordinary level of the General Certificate of Education, the Certificate of Secondary Education and other external examinations. Pupils will be able at the age of sixteen to transfer to other secondary schools serving the area, i.e., Ashton Grammar School, Queen Eleanor's School for Girls and Kingsbury School, to follow courses leading to the Advanced level of the General Certificate or to the College of Further Education in Dunstable. Provision has also been made so that the school may take its place as the centre for further education in the area.

Did You Know?

Manor House
Men who have lived at the Manor House include Simon de Montfort, Sir Neil Loving (hero of Sir Arthur Conan Doyle's novel, *The White Company*), Earl Stafford and Lord Wentworth. A constant visitor was the Duke of Monmouth.

Town or Village
Many older residents refer to Toddington as a town and resent it being called a village. In the bye-laws there is a reference to 'the Town Pump on the village Green'.
  The pond, which is now the Memorial Gardens, was once the Town Pond and the Town Hall, which still stands, has been converted into offices.

Market
A market was established by Royal Warrant in 1218. The market is stated to have been, in its prime, one of the largest in the county. In 1681 no fewer than 16 butchers held stands in the Square.

Visitors
In 1563 and 1576, Queen Elizabeth visited Lord Cheney at Toddington Manor. Shortly after Lord Cheney's death, his widow entertained King James and his Queen; and Thomas Archer, rector of Houghton Conquest, preached before them in St George's Church on 24 July 1608. It has also been reported that Charles I visited Toddington, and Charles II is said to have passed through on his way from Worcester.

Methodist Church
The first lighting was by candles. Next came oil lamps, followed in 1863 by gas. The gas became very unsatisfactory and everyone was delighted when electricity was installed in the church in 1931.

Town Hall
In 1972 the parish council's view, backed by the majority of Toddington residents, was that the Town Hall was ugly and a white elephant. It was however saved from demolition by the Department of the Environment and was sold. The new owner restored this building and turned it into offices.

W.G. Grace
In the early 1900s the famous cricketer, W. G. Grace, attended cricket parties held every summer by Bob Sievier at Toddington Park.

The Social Club
Toddington Social Club, which stands on the corner of Luton Road and the High Street, was used in the 19th century for the manufacture of beer. By the beginning of this century this was discontinued and although still known locally as the Brewery, the building was used by a corn chandler for the storage of corn.

Roads
Dunstable Road used to be called Towns End. Park Road used to be called Parsons

End and Luton Road was Fins Lane. Tanners End owes its origins to a boggy field that was once full of tan-pits.

First World War
For several weeks when the blackberries were ripe, schoolchildren were allowed half-days from school to pick them. Vast amounts were gathered to make jam for soldiers, for which the children were paid about a farthing a pound. Instead of staying at school until they were 14, those boys who wanted to do agricultural work were allowed to leave at the age of 12.

Sunday School Treat
For many people in the early part of this century, the Sunday School treat was the highlight of the year. Children, parents and friends could go. Many teachers and officials took the day off from their work in order to help organise the event. For many this was their only day's holiday, apart from bank holidays, which they took. Places visited varied each year, but as transport was by horse and waggonette only short distances could be travelled, to local beauty spots such as Wardown Park and Dunstable Downs.

Skating
In the days before television during the winter, the most popular pastime, ice permitting, was ice skating on the clay pits at Fancott or at Higg's overflow, which was a flooded field about a mile and a half along the Harlington Road. It was not unusual to see two or three generations of the same family skating together.

Council Houses
The first council houses were built in 1923 in Dunstable Road on the site known as Stranger's Field. Eight houses were built.

The Pump
Many houses around the Market Square had no water supply of their own; water was obtained from a pump in the middle of the Green.

The Black Death
The Black Death was a highly infectious, often fatal disease which is reckoned to have wiped out at least a third of the population on the Continent and in England. This plague was no respector of persons. In 1349 before 4 January, the rector, Geoffrey de Sewenestre, had died of the plague and been replaced by a successor. As the year wore on, the temperature increased and so did the deaths. By the end of the year, three Toddington rectors had died.

The Frieze
St George's Church has an unusual exterior frieze below the cornice of the north side of the church. Now much worn by wind and weather, this 16th century frieze comprises some sixty grotesque figures. These figures include peacocks, greyhounds, a fox, a wyvern, a griffin and a sow and her litter. Local legend has it that this latter figure provided the name for the pub opposite – namely the *Sow and Pigs*.

Catholic Church
During the Second World War a number of Poles came to Toddington and the

surrounding district. They had nowhere to celebrate Mass so Miss Hopwood, a convert to Catholicism, turned the hall of her house Withington's in Park Road into a chapel, special permission having been granted for her to have the Mass in her own home.

Cow Warden

This unusual job came about because a herd of cows used the public footpath between the old school and Conger Lane. The cows used to frighten the children so a cow warden was appointed. The first warden was 'Diggles' Hucklesby, who appeared on the television programme What's My Line and nobody could guess his job. His certificate hung for many years in his favourite pub, the *Sow and Pigs*. Tom Brown succeeded Diggles. Apart from preventing the cows frightening the children, the footpath had to be kept clear and the muck shifted.

Harold Fletcher

Milkman Harold Fletcher is dedicated to his milkround. So much so that when his former boss for 28 years, Fred Ireland, left Harold the choice of 'My milk round or £500' in his will in 1981, Harold put his customers first. 'I've been doing it for so long, I'd just like to see it kept going,' he said.

Sidney Vass

Sidney Vass was a parcels carrier who, in his four-wheeled van drawn by a heavy horse, used to carry parcels to and from Harlington Station. He was involved in carting blackberries to the station. Women would start at four o'clock in the morning picking blackberries at Coxley Bushes and Daintry Wood. They had to be weighed and loaded onto 'Siddy' Vass's trolley. The blackberries were used for making dye and had to arrive in London the same day as picked.

Bell Foundry

There was a bell-foundry at Toddington. The Ruffords were a family of bell makers who carried on their business from the 14th to the 16th century. Bells cast by the Ruffords can be found in several churches in Bedfordshire, Buckinghamshire and other counties.

Oak Apple Day

The church bells used to be rung on 'Oak Apple' or Restoration Day (29 May) and boughs of oak were placed at the doors of local residents by the ringers who, later in the day, called back 'for their gratuities'.

The Passing Bell

The 'passing bell' used to declare by the number of strokes the sex of the deceased person: three for a man, two for a woman and one for a child.

Bernard Hyde MBE

In the 1992 Queen's New Year's Honours, Bernard Hyde, of Meadow Road, was awarded the MBE for his services to the public and community in Bedfordshire. Bernard, affectionately known as Bim, has been a member of Toddington Parish Council for 42 years.

The Odd Two Inches
St George's Church is 103 ft 2 ins long. The chancel is 36 ft 2 ins by 18 ft 2 ins and the nave is 21 ft 2 ins wide.

The Parvise
This building dates from the 15th century when it was originally used as a chapel and living quarters for the parish priest. It is rare because of its two spiral staircases, one from the church and one from the churchyard, which meet as they ascend. It is also unusual for a building of this kind to be attached to the church. The top room of the three-roomed building was used as an armoury during the Napoleonic War.

Bedfordshire Clangers
Most people have heard of this dish but very few today have experienced the joys of eating it. Agricultural workers used to eat it for lunch. It's a largish suet roll with meat at one end and jam at the other end. A Toddington WI member recalled that when she was a child, her mother used to make clangers in the traditional way: 'We used to eat the meaty bit first with vegetables and then the jammy bit with custard afterwards.'

Kelly's Directory 1940

PRIVATE RESIDENTS

Baker Wilfred E. Watson, 10 Park rd
Barclay Capt. Robert (late RFA), Denbigh house
Biddlecombe Fredk. Spring vale
Bligh Arthur, 70 Dunstable road
Clarke Mrs. Hill, Meadowland, Leighton road
Cooke Percy John, Dunstan house
Douglas Miss Margt. Toddington park
Dunham Miss, 45 High street
Fawcett Ralph FM, DSO, CM, MD, JP, Conger house
Hollingworth Frederick Charles, Burham house, Dunstable road
Hopwood Miss B.C. Wythingtons, Park road
Horley Misses, 11 Park road
Hunt Rev. Francis Whittaker MA (rector), Denbigh house
Lambton Lieut.-Comdr. Hedworth, RN(ret), Toddington hill
Lindeloo Jacob Anton, Sundial cottage, Market square
Murray Donald Ivan Dewar, Lodge farm
Nicholl Miss, 29 Leighton road
Owen Rev. Baldwin H. (Methodist), The Manse, Leighton road
Seebohm Derrick, 61 Station rd
Skinner Col. Edward John DSO, JP, Toddington manor
Smith Mrs. Emily, Willow Spring
Turvey William, The Retreat

COMMERCIAL

Ablett Thos. farmer, Warmark
Allen G. H. & Sons, plumbers & glaziers, 24 High st. T N 210
Allen Fredk. Geo. boot repr. Chalton
Andrews Rd. Oakley, farmer, Cross farm, Chalton
Angel Inn (Mrs. Lizzie Randall), 1 Luton rd
Ashby Alice Mary (Miss), statnr. & post office, 3 Church sq.
Atzema Stanley R. chemist, 6 Station rd. T N 259
Barclays Bank Ltd. (sub-branch, open on thurs. 11 a.m. to 1 p.m.), 2 High st; head office, 54 Lombard st. London E C 3
Barnes, Richardson & Furber, physicians & surgns. (attend), 21 Dunstable rd
Bedford Arms P H. (Mrs. Louisa Rowe), 62 High st
Bell P.H.(Wm. Ayres), Market sq
Beloff Simon, farmer, Red Hills farm, T N 280
Benning & Hoare, solctrs. (attend 1st & 3rd fri. in month 1.15 to 3 p.m.)
Bird Bros. poultry farmers, Chalton. T N 323
Bolter Edwin J. gamekeeper to Col. E.J. Skinner DSO, JP
Boutwood Aubrey, solicitor & commissioner for oaths (firm, Thornley & Boutwood)
Brentnall & Cleland Ltd. coal mers. 43 High st
Briden Bros. butchers, 23 Church sq T N 235
Briden T. & Sons, bldrs. 44 High st. T N 216
Brittain Rd Chas, cycle dlr. Luton rd
Bryant Frank, shopkpr & post office T N 265
Buckingham Chas. smallholder, Princes st
Buckingham Leonard Jn. farmer, Gas st & butcher, 11 Market sq. T N 314
Buckingham Regnld. C. W. farmer, Crowbush
Buckingham Ronald Ward, haulage contractor 37 Dunstable rd T N 285
Candelent Leonard Alfd. haulage contactor, Gas st. T N 205
Carr Albt. butcher, 14 Market sq. T N 233
Carr Rt. Geo. farmer, Fancott. T N 211
Chamberlain Jsph. Wm. grocer, 23 Station rd
Childs Hrbt. dairyman, Briarmeade dairy. T N 254
Childs Jn. travelling draper, 49 High st
Childs Wm Arth. shopkeeper. 20 High st
Clarke Wm. chimney sweeper, 18 Station rd
Cleaver Bros. confctnrs. 26 High st
Cleaver Bernard Geo. insur. agt. 55 Dunstable rd
Clifford Frdk. & Son, bakers, 7 Market sq
Consumers' Tea Co. Ltd. grocers, Market sq. T N 209
Cosy (Touring Talkie Picture Co.), Gas st
Crawley Leonard, butcher, 17 Market sq
Dean Chas. smallholder, 23 Park rd
Evans Alfd. wheelwright, 17 Dunstable rd
Fancott Arms. P.H. (Jn. Wm Stringer), Fancott
Fawcett Ralph FM, DSO, MD, CMMcGill, LRCP & S.Edin., JP, physcn. & surgn. & medical officer & public vaccinator Toddington district, Ampthill Area Hockliffe district, Luton Area Guardians Committees & certifying factory surgn. Conger ho. T N 202
Fleckney Christopher. motor engnr. Station rd. T N 231
Fox Edgar Hattill, saddler, 21 Church sq
Franklin Chas. shopkpr. 5 Princes st
George Sydney, boot repr. 68 High st
Giles A & Sons, haulage contactrs. 59 High st. T N 343
Graham Chas. carrier, 50 High st
Greengrass Doris Violet (Mrs.), grocer, 16 High st
Griffin P.H. (Eric Sam. Wickens), Station rd
Hanson Jn. Wm shopkpr. 9 Luton rd
Hardwick Regnld. D. dentist (attends thurs. by appointment), 62 High st
Hart G. & Son, newsagts. 6 High st
Hawes Elijah Jas. & Son, boot mkrs. 10 High st
Hawes Chas. Rd. nurseryman, Dunstable rd
Heath Harry, farmer, Happyland
Highnam Norman H. dairy farmer, Old Park
Hobbs Geo. butcher, 2 Dunstable rd
Hobbs Jas. head gardener to Col E. J. Skinner DSO, JP, Park rd
Holman Harry, blacksmith, 37 Station rd
Holman Sydney, plumber, 12 Dunstable rd
Horley Kimberwell, insr. agt. 4 Park rd
Ireland Fredk. dairy farmer, Fancott
Kempton Wm. Fras. Jn. cycle agt. 18 High st
Kingham George, poultry breeder & dealer. Fancott
Lane Harry, smallholder, 68 Dunstable rd
Little Jesse & Sons, nurserymen. T N 217
Luton Industrial Co-operative Society Ltd. grocers, Luton rd. T N 247
Luton Gas Co. High st. T N 263
Marlow Eliz. Ann (Mrs.), farmer, Fancott
Marlow Jsph. cowkeeper, Luton rd
Marlow Wm. farmer, Dropshort farm
Marriott Algernon Cromwell, farmer, Herne Poplars farm. T N 239
Martin Austin Edwd. dairy farmer, Herne Dairy farm
Moore Geo. hairdressr. 10 Station rd
Mountfort Chas. grocer, 60 High st. T N 242
Mountfort Ronald, hairdresser, 30 High st.

Muckleston Wm. butcher, 6 Market sq
Nag's Head P.H. (Ernest Capell), 16 Station rd
National Deposit Friendly Society (Beds & Hunts divsn) (Alec C. Crees, sec.), 40 Princes st
Oddfellows' Arms P.H. (Chas. M. Jeeves), 2 Gas st
Oliver Edwd. Geo. market gardener, Dicton, Bradford rd
Pateman Geo Thos. market gardener, 42 Dunstable rd
Patrick G. J. & Co. dairy farmers, Herne Willow farm
Pett Bros. motor engnrs. T N 245
Pilgrim Evan Owen, wheelwright, 17 High st
Randall Thomas & Harry, market gardeners, 86 Dunstable rd
Randall Fras. Wm. baker, 22 High st
Randall Thos. blacksmith, Luton rd
Red Lion P.H. (Cyril Kingham), 22 Market sq
Rigg & Leggettt, farmers, Alma farm, Leighton rd. T N 300
Rowe Wltr. Fredk. smallholder, 4 Luton rd
Ruffett Alfd. Chas. cycle agt. 11 Station rd
Russell H. C. & Son, smallholders, Leighton rd
Russell Chas. Hy. shopkpr. 83 Dunstable rd
Sales Edwd. fishmng. 15 Market sq
Scrivener Geo. farmer, Herne grn & Herne Manor farm T N 238
Seymour & Son, carpntrs. 21 Market sq
Sharp Frank, printer, 26 Princes st
Sow & Pigs Hotel (Mrs. Florence Emily Innell, proprietress), 19 Church sq T N 214
Stanghon Harry, farmer, Herne grange
Star P.H., (Chas. Hy. Tayler), Chalton
Thornley & Boutwood, solicitors
Toddington Conservative & Unionist Club (A.C. Cress, sec.), 1 High st
Toddington Workmen's Social Club & Institute (W.T. Hair, hon. sec.), High st. T N 228
Walhert Mary D. (Mrs.), grocer, 38 Market sq. T N 261
Walker Arth. & Sons, bakers,12 High Street T N 321
Ward Geo & Sons, farmers, Manor farm & Common farm, Chalton T N 282
Ward Fredk. poultry dlr. Chalton
Wild Algernon Gordon, farmer, Mill farm. T N 266
Wilkinson Jn. draper, 21 High st
Williamson P. & M. (Misses), fancy drapers, 8 High st
Williamson Mrs. corsetiére, 43 High st
Willison Sydney J. tailor, 32 High st

Roll of Honour

Names on the Roll of Honour in St George's Church, Toddington, of the men who died in the First and Second World Wars:

1914 – 1918

Edward Aldred
Wilfred Allen
John Ansell
George Baker
John Baker
Alfred Bennett
Ernest Brazier
Sidney Bright
Albert Buckingham
George Buckingham
William Buckingham
Arthur Buckingham
Thomas Carr
Joseph Chance
Sidney Chance
George Clarke
Richard Childs
Charles Coles
Fred Coles
G. Coles
John Coles
Stanley Coles
Arthur Cope
Thomas Cousins

Frank Denton
Frank Fane
Samuel Fleckney
Hubert Fossey
Harry Franklin
Sidney Franklin
W. Fuller
Wilfrid Gobby
Alec Gordon
George Harris
John Hart
Reginald Hart
Charles Hobbs
William Horley
Fred Hucklesby
J. Hucklesby
Sidney Hucklesby
John Hurst
William Hyde
George Ireland
A. King
Arthur Kingham
Albert Lane
Chris Larkin

Cecil Muckleston
George Muckleston
Harold Muckleston
William Muckleston
Albert Osborne
Major Pateman
William Pateman
William Peach
William Purser
William Randall
Harry Rhodes
Hugh Shepherd
George Smith
Sidney Smith
Thomas Smith
William Smith
William Stanton
Leonard Stimpson
H. Sylvester
Harry Walters
Frederick Whitbread

1939 – 1945

Henry Atkinson
Arthur Bates
Ernest Bonner
Frederick Bottrill
Ronald Briden
Kenneth Chance
George Day
Frederick Dennis
Reginald Denton

Reginald Hancox
Stanley Horning
Frank Janes
Dennis Muckleston
Leonard Norton
Daniel Paterson
Robert Paterson
Walter Peckham
Peter Sears

Richard Shelton
Edward Skinner
John Skinner
Frederick Willison